Scottish Ballad In The Eighteenth Century: A Bibliographical Study

Mackenzie, Mabel Laura Hunter

THE SCOTTISH BALLAD IN THE EIGHTEENTH CENTURY:

A BIBLIOGRAPHICAL STUDY

M. Laura Mackenzie

A thesis submitted in partial fulfilment of

the requirements for the degree of

DOCTOR OF PHILOSOPHY

in the Department

of

ENGLISH

The University of Toronto

UNIVERSITY OF TORONTO
SCHOOL OF GRADUATE STUDIES

PROGRAMME OF THE FINAL ORAL EXAMINATION
FOR THE DEGREE OF DOCTOR OF PHILOSOPHY

of

MABEL LAURA HUNTER MACKENZIE

11 00 A M   SATURDAY, OCTOBER 22nd 1955
AT 44 HOSKIN AVENUE

THE SCOTTISH BALLAD IN THE EIGHTEENTH CENTURY

A BIBLIOGRAPHICAL STUDY

COMMITTEE IN CHARGE

Professor J R O'Donnell Chairman
Professor A S P Woodhouse
Professor W D B Grant
Professor J R MacGillivray
Professor C W Dunn
Professor K MacLean
Professor L K Shook
Professor P A Child
Professor R M Saunders

Professor W H Clawson

lad in the
nto three
nterest
 significant
c sensibility.
diffusion of
 of the
cy himself,
inally
nown, but
ste or
in her scope.
e a judgment
 best.

X the utility
th century
wo ballads,
well's Lament.'
y of the first,
that her
on ballads.

 Such a
and has long
 the material
sing it. It

- is an
and accordingly
fulfilling
phy.

BIOGRAPHICAL

1900   --Born Uplanmoor Scotland
1945   --B A , University of British Columbia
1947   --M A., University of British Columbia
1946-48 --Lecturer, University of British Columbia
1950-56 --Instructor, University of British Columbia
1948-50)
1954-55) --School of Graduate Studies, University of Toronto

THESIS

The Scottish Ballad in the Eighteenth Century
A Bibliographical Study

(ABSTRACT)

The purpose of this thesis is to make some contribution to the study of the collecting, editing and printing of ballads an activity which holds an important place
in the literary history of the eighteenth century   Although chronological limits
frequently impose arbitrary restrictions not only undesirable but inaccurate the
limit is here justified by three facts   first, that for a hundred years before the
beginning of the eighteenth century Scottish ballads existed only in manuscript, in
broadsides or in the memories of a few men and women, and no systematic collecting had as yet begun and secondly that early in the nineteenth century the
terms of the problem altogether changed with the introduction of modern methods
of scholarship which governed the transcribing of ballads and precluded the activity of "editing" as the eighteenth century conceived it   Thirdly during the period
1740-1780 the editing and polishing of ballads by talented, frequently anonymous
poets re-shaped folk-tradition into literature with the result that many of our
finest ballads were printed in their most beautiful form at this time   The restriction of attention to the Scottish ballads was necessary if the degree of thoroughness
desirable were to be achieved. This restriction may be further justified on grounds
of the intrinsic merit and historical importance of the Scottish ballads and by the
fact that a fruitful field of research (for a critic with a sound knowledge of the various Scottish dialects) would be the examination of the eighteenth-century versions

Though much valuable work has already been done in ballad study, the thesis
breaks new ground   first by supplying a check-list of the printing of Scottish ballads
in the eighteenth century secondly by examining in detail the textual variants in
the printed versions of two important specimens, and, thirdly, by tracing with
the help of the prefaces introductory notes and dissertations included in the collections, and of published correspondence, the aims and methods of the principal editors of Scottish ballads   The thesis falls into three parts

In the first part (chapters i - iii) it provides a survey of the increasing interest
in ballads in the eighteenth century, of the work and methods of ballad collectors
before 1765 (the year of the publication of Reliques of Ancient English Poetry) of
Percy himself and of the other great collectors, Herd and Ritson   The first collector to be discussed is James Watson editor of the important Choice Collection of
Comic and Serious Scots Poems But the emphasis naturally falls on the work of
Allan Ramsay in his Tea-Table Miscellany and Ever Green, on the aims and methods
of Percy and his friend, the poet William Shenstone and on the part played by
David Dalrymple Lord Hailes, and by David Herd the Scottish antiquarian, and
finally on the approximation to a more rigorously scholarly procedure by Joseph
Ritson, the English collector as revealed in his own collections, and in his critical
strictures on Percy and on the collections of John Pinkerton which achieved more
popularity than their merit warranted A brief survey is also given of the various
collections and printings made in the last three decades of the century   Part I
serves a the necessary introduction to Part II where the methods of these editors
are exemplified in detail, and also to Part III, where their collections repeatedly
recur

The second part (chapters iv and v) is given to an exhaustive study of the printed versions of two ballads "Captain Car or Edom O Gordon" and "Lady Anne Bothwell's Lament' "Edom O Gordon', to give the ballad its best-known title was chosen for several reasons first it appears to be a ballad of minstrel origin, secondly, it is one of the first dated ballads to describe an incident in Scottish history, and thirdly, it affords a very fine example of the editorial methods of Percy, Shenstone and Dalrymple who all added if not what Menéndez Pidal calls "la belleza más alta", at least a great many typical eighteenth-century touches "Lady Anne Bothwell's Lament" was chosen because both its subject matter and its history have been much discussed with each ballad editor in turn giving his version of both text and history The purpose here is not only to illustrate in detail the methods adopted by the editors of whom a general account has already been given and thus to substantiate the conclusions reached but to afford a specimen of the kind of bibliographical research that is necessary for the principal ballads if we are to form a complete idea of collecting and editing in the century as a whole

The third part, presented as an extended appendix to the discussion in Parts I and II, consists of a check-list of the eighteenth-century printings of those Scottish ballads which occur in Child's great collection, The English and Scottish Popular Ballads and of a few others which he does not include, the term "Scottish ballad" being here interpreted to embrace all ballads with a Scottish variant or portion of a variant Although it is more than a hundred years since Svend Grundtvig the great Danish collector, announced that he intended to follow the procedure advocated by William Motherwell in his Minstrelsy 1827, and print all the texts of ballads he found available, and although literary historians have long been aware of the changes which have taken place in the history of a ballad from one generation to the next or indeed from one editor to another, such a procedure has not been followed by collectors of Scottish ballads, except in cases where isolated ballads have been studied Thus it is believed that a check-list of this kind is a valuable and indeed indispensable instrument for a complete investigation of the subject It is, moreover, an excellent indication of the vogue and diffusion of Scottish ballads in the eighteenth century The temper of the age was increasingly favourable to ballads and popular songs, as the many collections and printings testify

Since the aim in Part III is merely to provide sufficient description to secure certain identification, the Check-List consists of catalogue entries the title of the work, the name of the editor the place of publication and the date if these are available, and the name of the library in which a copy of the work is to be found

lad in the
nto three
nterest
significant
c sensibility.
diffusion of
of the
cy himself,
inally
nown, but
ste or
in her scope.
e a judgment
best.

X the utility
ith century
wo ballads,
well's Lament.'
y of the first,
that her
on ballads.

Such a
and has long
the material
sing it. It

- is an
and accordingly
fulfilling
phy.

Mrs M. Laura Mackenzie's thesis, The Scottish Ballad in the Eighteenth Century: A Bibliographical Study, falls into three parts. The first is concerned with the increasing interest taken in the ballad during the eighteenth century, a significant indication of the change from neo-classic to romantic sensibility Mrs Mackenzie concentrates almost entirely upon the diffusion of the ballad by describing the practice and intentions of the important ballad collectors - Watson and Ramsay, Percy himself, Herd, Ritson and Pinkerton. She suefully but unoriginally gathers together and relates much that was already known, but she fails to proceed to any general discussion of taste or literary theory, a task that should have fallen within her scope. On the few occasions when she does hesitantly venture a judgment on these issues, her opinions are disputable, at the best.

The second part attempts to justify XXXXXXXXXXXX the utility of her check list of ballads printed in the eighteenth century by carefully tracing the history of XXXXXXXXXXX two ballads, 'Captain Car, or, Edom o Gordon' and 'Lady Anne Bothwell's Lament Her treatment of both these ballads, but particularly of the firs is excellent, and proves beyond doubt her contention that her check list could be invaluable to any critic engaged on ballads.

The third part consists of the check list itself. Such a list does not exist, and the need for one is obvious and has long been felt, and the present one conveniently presents the material in such a way that t'ere could be no difficulty in using it. It also represents a deal of research and labour.

The thesis - at least the second and third parts - is an original and important contribution to scholarship, and according I recommend that it should be accepted as partially fulfilling the requirements for the degree of Doctor of Philosophy.

TABLE OF CONTENTS

PART I

Chapter one

INTRODUCTION

Seldom in the history of literature has so slender
a body of work roused so much controversy and speculation
as the collection of short poems known as the English and
Scottish ballads.   Controversy begins immediately an
attempt is made to define the term, "ballad".[1] Of a score
of definitions the one given by Gerould seems most apt, since
it includes the three regularly recurring qualities found in
all ballads: "A ballad is a folksong that tells a story
with stress on the crucial situation, tells it by letting
the action unfold itself in event and speech, and tells it
objectively with little comment or intrusion of personal
bias."[2] It may be pointed out here that "folksong"
requires further definition, but this in turn would involve
a discussion of oral transmission, and this kind of transmission
in its pure form has hardly existed in England or Scotland
for the last four hundred and fifty years, while there is little
recorded history of ballads before the sixteenth century.
According to Gummere a ballad is "a narrative poem without
any known author or any marks of individual authorship such
as sentiment and reflection, meant, in the first instance,
for singing, and connected, as its name implies, with the

communal ance, but attai te to a process of oral tradition among peo le free from literary influences and fairly ho ogeneous."[3] Hodgart, while acnc le ing the difficulty of efining a ball a, nevertheless aumr tes certain stylistic characteristics which distinguish a ballad from any other kind of poem:

The story moves orward in bounds, ag inst a b c round of regular stanzaic melo y and against the formal ttern-ing of folk art: the re etitions in threes and severs and the conventional phr ses. The ra idity and viole ce of the action is all the more striking bec u e of the ecorum nd formality m int ined in the b il s. Gummere h s well described their movement as "leaping nd lingering".
        The main end of the b ll ds is to re ent the story ramatically, n t e efore x l nation, mor list comment, and even original hr eology re u ress. Unconventional metaphors re rare, e a s bec u e t ey might hold u the narrative . . . . The b ll s u e their own peculiar rhetoric and oetic iction to incr se the dr matic re sure . . . . The ball s are sternly economic l in their vocabul ry . . . . . Another rhetorical device is "arallelism in hr e nd i ea", as Gerould c lls it, nd the favourite y of evelo ing this arallelism is by increment l re etition. E ch stanza repeats the one before it, ut ith some iltion ich leads on to the clim x . . . . Yet aroth r evice is the apu rently irrelev nt re rain.[4]

The stuly of this elusive form, this "h nu ul of simple nd s len id poetry"[5], has now become a m tter or uch rigorous methods of inve tigation that Be ttie, the Scottish b ll d editor, wher he recently ub ished his anthology of bor er b ll s, ound it necess ry to ex lain that he was not a s ecialist on the su ject.[6] Ho g rt, at the beginning of his B ll , ublished in 1950, as

equally modest, must tell that what he offers is merely
"a guide to jungle territory: at most it may be able to
point out some of the main features of the landscape."[7]

The assumption is frequently made that so much is
known about ballads that little remains to be learned. A
greater misapprehension of the facts, however, could
hardly be imagined. According to Hustvedt in his Ballad
Books and Ballad Men:

Collectors, editors, commentators, scholars as a body have
indeed immensely widened our knowledge. Bishop Percy was
a tyro as compared ith a reasonably well-informed student
of today. Yet sweeping conclusions are even now hardly
warranted. Many special studies must still be undertaken
in order to test the older generalizations and possibly
to erect new ones. The hesitant investigator may take
heart in the conviction that though the sheaves have been
pretty carefully gleaned from the fields, the threshing is
only well begun.[8]

One area of ballad study has already been against cinely
explored, that of the origin of ballads, and it is unlikely
that much can be added to the information gathered from
exhaustive enquiries. All evidence points to a multiplicity
of origins and sources. Ifor Evans, however, gives some
idea of the grain still to be garnered when he says of the
words of "Corpus Christi" (designated both as ballad and
carol), that they "give opportunity for every type of
learned criticism; the philologist can use them, the
literary historian, the historian of tendencies, of form,
and the psychological and philosophic critic."[9] A similar
claim (

Hodgart touches specifically on a branch of this criticism:

It is . . . possible to interpret many of the images that appear in the ballads as psychoanalytical "symbols", that is, as examples of an unconscious translation of a psychological situation into indirect terms. Freud and Jung have made us familiar with this kind of symbolism and have traced parallels between the images of dreams and those of folklore. It is not difficult to apply their interpretations to such a stanza as this:

> For forty days and forty nights
> He rode thro/tlule to the knee,
> And he saw neither sun nor moon,
> But heard the roaring of the sea.[10]

While criticism of this kind does not come within the scope of this thesis, the assumption upon which the present study is based is that detailed research must be undertaken into the variants of any particular ballad to provide solutions to problems of historical, aesthetic, anthropological and critical interest arising out of ballad study. What is attempted here is simply a bibliography of publications printed in the eighteenth century -- the important century for ballad collectors -- which contain versions of Scottish ballads. Since the aim of the bibliographer is to investigate the material means of written communication, in order to provide such description of the physical features of the work investigated as to secure identification, this compilation consists of simple catalogue entries: the title of the work, the name of the editor, the place of publication, the date, and the name of the library in   of

the kind at present exists. A.E. Case's _Bibliography of English Poetic Miscellanies, 1521-1750_ ends before ballad collectors, in the sense of ballad editors, began to publish the results of their labours. Up to the present the listing of sources in J.C. Dick's _The Songs of Robert Burns_, 1903, which has been heavily leant upon by writers in this field, remains the most complete list of its kind for Scottish ballad literature. It is, however, highly specialized, and gives only the sources for ballads which were adapted by Burns.

A study of this kind has entailed an examination of the methods used by eighteenth-century editors and collectors in presenting their findings to the public, and the results of this examination will occupy the first part of my thesis. Literary historians have long been aware of the changes which have taken place in the history of a ballad from one generation to the next, or indeed, from one editor to another. Investigation of some of these changes in the printed ballad has, to quote A. Watkin-Jones, proved "popular literary sport" since the publication in 1867 of the folio MS. used by Thomas Percy in the compiling of his _Reliques of Ancient English Poetry_, 1765. Of great importance here is the examination of eighteenth-century correspondence to illuminate early methods of ballad editing.
Hans He

Manuscri ts, in which he u ed lett rs by Thom s ercy, Joseph Ritson, David Herd, Lord Hailes, George P ton nd others to s ow what ha ened to old songs t the han s of editors ith a esire to im rove, nd conver ely th t t e old songs ere like befcre t e bre th of ei l t erth-c tury good t ste blew u on t em. In 19 9 he ublished Thom s P rcy un Willi n Sh rstone, a corres on ence hich throws light not only on e iting, but on some con tempor ry t ste in poetry, nd not a little illumin tion on cert in liter ry ju gments of the day. Hecht ubli hed only art of the voluminous correspon ence betr een the t o men, but the part w s enough to show herstone's erthusi stic agreement ith Percy's met o s, nd t eir utter lack of interest in textual accur cy as a stand rd to be i ve . Nowhere does one fin objections on the p rt of eit er to ch nging, amen ing, or revising any b ll d to m e it con-orm to contempor ry t ste, "the t ste", s id Shenstone, which "is some h t higher th n its genius". Shenstone's letters h ve since b en e ited by inc n Mall m in 1 39 an by Marjorie illia s in the s me ye r. The public tion of co respon ence continues ith The P rcy Let ers by D. Nichol Smith and Cle nth Erooks s gener l editors, ork which is still in rogress. The art layed ty henstone as an e itor is con irmed by the ublic tion in 1952 of henston ' in

New Zealand, where n interesting example/disclosed of what
happened to a b llad at the hands of three different editors
in the same period. The Miscellany contains a hitherto
unpublished variant of the much edited "Adom O Gordon",
collated with Percy's version. (See below, p. 83)

William Motherwell is acknowledged to have been the
first ballad editor to stress explicitly the importance of
examining all variants of a ballad. In 1827 he wrote in
the introduction to his Minstrelsy:

Of every old traditionary ballad known, there exists h t
may be c lled different versions. In other words, the same
story is told after a different fashion in one district of
the country, from what it is remembered in another. It
therefore not infrequently occurs, th t no two copies
obtained in parts of the country distant from each other
will be found completely to tally in their texts; perhaps
they may not have a single stanza which is mutual roperty,
exce t certain commonplaces which seem an integrant ortion
of the original mechanism of all our ancient b ll ds, and
the presence of which forms one of their most peculiar and
distinctive characteristicks, as contrasted with the modern
ballad. Both of these copies, however, narr to the same
story. In that articular, their identity with e ch other
cannot be disputed; but in many minute circumst nces, as
well as in the way by which the s me c tastrophe is brought
out, sensible differences exist . . . .
All versions of a ballad so preserved by oral transmission from one age to another, are entitled to be considered as of equal authenticity and coeval production, one
with the other, although among them, wi e and irreconcilable
discrepancies exist.[11]

Motherwell adopted the procedure ne advoc ted, and
his example has been closely follo ed. In 1853 Svend
Grundtvig announced in his lan, a ros ectus setting forth
his principles for the proper editing of b ll ds in his

Danmarks Gamle Folkeviser, that he intended to adhere to
Motherwell's standards and print all the texts of ballads
he found available.[12] In 1857 F.J. Child in turn
referred to Grundtvig's collection as "a work which has
no equal in its line, and which may/serve as a model for
collections of National Ballads."[13] Child also stated that
work such as Grundtvig's "can only be imitated by an
English editor, never equalled, for the material is not
to hand."[14] Nevertheless Child did not follow Grundtvig's
example and print all valuable texts, nor did he explain
the principles by which he selected ballads and versions
for inclusion, though he occasionally gave reasons for
rejections. Kittredge declares that Child's method was
almost infallible. "A forged or retouched piece could not
deceive him for a moment; he detected the slightest jar in
the genuine ballad tone."[15] But Kittredge is not accurate
here, as many of Child's versions show signs of forging
and retouching. Therefore difference of opinion
regarding the qualities of various ballads is inevitable,
and the desirability of gaining all texts, whether
mutilated, miserably corrupt or debased, becomes apparent,
and the usefulness of the Check-list in Part III of this
thesis as a supplement to Child's volumes in ballad
study can be readily seen.

Examination of the Check-list will show that
poems a

 now ever, I point at the ... wh ...

an inclusion

such/ ...

In his final text, <u>The English and Scottish Popular Ballads,</u>
Child point ... ton ... tity v ... t, ... rt
... hid as ay's po ..., ... s ...
... oll ton, stating that ... new's r si ... s of ... popular
... ert r ... ... rt rinal rhy ... s .... In ... iti ...
its importance, ... d t ... lt ... ... in ... fe ...
... t t lens y ... to ... it fro ... h ol por ... ... t ... in l ...,
... hom h ... ot ... o ... to ... ist, ... iges t ... olt ... to b ...
m ... ... in lo t ... ... t t ... ... t ... t ... ... t ... g ... t ... tio ... l
v ... sions w ... pro ... bly ... row ... ... t t. I ... ot d
... tat R ... ... t ... tr ... ipt ... ... by b ... is in 17 ... ,
but did not ... ation ... v ... is of ... , in ... so ... ... son.

... d n ... rson, who, ... r ... ... ng to ... ... t, "h ... ... r
almost alone in ... taining ... r ... ght ... t ... tity v ... al ns
... ritically ... l with ... ... t ... lf ... t ... ...
... ottish v ... acul ..." a ... ... t ... ... th ... opinion t ... t ... n
... ulad is ... et it ... st ... it is ... rly o ... t ... r ... d in ...
... for ... it ... s ... r ... p ... ly ... t ... ltion. ... rh ps
... nd ... on' ... ... stu ... t t ... n of ... ... ld' ... ... ts ... ... r
be bas ... ... n ... p ... ... t ... ... t ... ... s of t ...

prosy and vulgar commonplace a fine ballad may sink, after a
few years' subjection to the standards of popular taste."

Henderson's criticism is valid in showing one
effect of transmission, that of debasing a ballad. But
there is another aspect. Popular taste does not always
propagate vulgarity and prosiness:

[U]na poesía tradicional . . . es el resultado de múltiples
creaciones individuales que se suman y entrecruzan, su
autor no puede tener nombre determinado, su nombre es
legión. Pero en esta creación poética colectiva, no hay
nada de abismal insondable o misterioso. El milagro de la
poetización en común se explica llana y simplemente con
sólo reconocer que las variantes no son accidente inútil
para el arte; son parte de la invención poética; la belleza
más alta se puede revelar no sólo al primer cantor sino a
cualquier recitador . . . .
          Esta poesía que se rehace en cada repetición que e
refunde en cada una de sus variantes, las cuales viven y se
propagan en ondas de carácter colectivo, a través de un
grupo humano y sobre un territorio determinado, es la
poesía propiamente <u>tradicional</u>, bien distinta de la otra
meramente <u>popular</u>.[20]

Although Menéndez Pidal is here discussing specifically
the matter of the spontaneous generation of beauty in oral
transmission, one may observe a similar aesthetic effect
when a ballad is transmogrified by an editor who is also
poetically endowed. Hodgart points to Goethe's adaptation
of "Heidenroslein" to show how the aesthetic re-shaping of
a traditional song has made it the standard version for
lieder singers. To illustrate this point, and also to show
the variation which exists among printed versions, two will
be collated, "Captain Car, or Edom O Gordon", and "Lady Anne

~~the~~ otuwel's Lament".

The usefulness of a study of this kind is not
limited, however, solely to ballad scholarship. In his preface to An Introduction to a Survey of Scottish Dialects,[21]
Professor Angus McIntosh speaks of the close organic
relationship the survey of dialects has with other
studies, particularly in the investigation of oral folk
traditions and material culture. Carrying the study of
ballads into the survey of dialects would be profitable for
the dialectologist, since in many of the older ballads the
use of the vernacular persisted longer than in any other
form. Some of the older words and idioms which had
vanished from the speech of even the illiterate countryman
in remote parts of Scotland, were retained in the oral
transmission of the ballad, so that Alan Ramsay, the
earliest ballad editor, had to supply "a Glossary, or an
explanation of the Scots words", albeit a very imperfect
glossary, when he issued his first small collection. Percy
followed Ramsay's example and compiled a glossary for his
Reliques, and moreover, gave the following advice to David
Herd, through George Paton, Herd's voluntary amenuensis, on
the subject of Herd's forthcoming second book of ballads:

Your notes should . . . illustrate any allusions to the old
manners, customs, opinions or idioms of the ancient Scotch
nation: These are now wearing out so fast, that, if not
preserved in such publications as these they will be utterly
unknown [22]

however, to retain the old vocabulary, just as the vernacular of each succeeding generation became less purely
Scottish than that of its predecessor, so did the vernacular in the printed versions of ballads tend to change
rapidly in the eighteenth century, and with, occasionally,
very curious results. Some editors, Percy, for example, in
their desire to halt this modernization produced an-
achronisms not only in the content of a ballad, but in its
vocabulary. Finally, it may be added that to show the
morphological peculiarities of a word in different places
and at different times, two great works in progress, The
Dictionary of the Older Scottish Tongue, and The Scottish
National Dictionary, frequently resort to ballads for
illustration and example.

Chapter two

BALLAD COLLECTORS BEFORE PERCY

At the beginning of the eighteenth century the
Scottish ballad existed only in manuscript, in broadsides,
or in the memories of a few men and women. The first
source was not readily accessible, or even widely known.
The second source often presented the ballad in a debased
version. The third source, that of oral transmission, was
as fallible as human memory. Thus when literary historians
tell us that in the year 1707, the year of the Union, Scotland had been without poetry in the Scottish tongue for a
hundred years, they mean that the Scottish people no longer
had even their ballads. "There was no life, no vitality, no
intellectual questionings in Scotland on the morrow of the
Union of 1707. Not merely was the auld sang ended; it
looked as if there might never be another."[1]   There is no
doubt that the "auld sang" was ended, but it is curious and
interesting that even in that aridity germination was taking
place. Before the end of the century ballads were being
heard in Scotland -- and few will deny that they are the
finest of all ballads -- the greatest vernacular poetry to
come out of Scotland was written, and "the first clearly

assignable impulse to the romantic movement of the eight-

eenth century" had been given by a Scotsman.

The words "first clearly assignable impulse" must

be taken at their face value. They do not mean that for

Allan Ramsay is claimed the role of progenitor of the

romantic movement, an honour which W.P. Ker believed was

earned by Sir William Temple half a century earlier:

Sir William Temple begins the modern sort of literary study
which looks for suggestion in old remote and foreign
regions, and he sets a precedent for the explorations of
various romantic schools, wandering through all the world
in search of plots, scenery and local colour.[3]

Or gently indicated for William Collins by Professor

Woodhouse: "Sometimes one is tempted to think of Collins

as the first of the romantics."[4] As Bernbaum pointed out,

the differences between the age of Pope and that of Words-

worth are not quite so clear-cut and distinct as literary

historians used to assume, nor is the passage from the

earlier period to the later abrupt and revolutionary:

The true history of the change is complicated; it illustrates
the general principle that mankind usually advances ty steps
which are hesitant and meandering. Few of the Pre-Romantics
understood fully in what new directions they were wandering.
They rarely used the word Romanticism; nor they resisted
the rise of Romanticism only partially or superficially, or
with respect to merely one or two restricted subjects or
phases.[5]

The restricted subject or phase contributing much to the

beginnings of the romantic movement, with which Allan

Ramsay is identified, is the revival of the Scottish ballad,

and he is here considered in regard to the part he played

in "stepping back into the Times that are past, and that

exit no more."[6]

Two widely disparate factors were at work in

Scotland at the beginning of the eighteenth century. The

Union brought on the one hand a desire to assimilate the

manners, customs, and,most important here, the speech of

the more powerful nation. The assimilation of English

speech has come about very slowly, but it had its begin-

nings immediately after the Union, and the same problem

arose which faces modern _makars_ today:

The poet in Scotland has some peculiar advantage, and
some peculiar difficulties. Both stem from the fact that
he has to make a deliberate choice as to what language he
is going to write in -- a choice between English nd
Lallans, or in some cases between English, Lallans and
Gaelic. He might be envied for this kind of ambidexterity,
and for his ability to produce effects in one language which
are not possible in another . . . . Certainly the liveli-
ness and piquancy of the present-day situation come from
this clash of possibilities, and no one will deny that good
poetry has been written in Scotland in more than one tongue
during these first thirty years of the Scottish Renascence
movement. Yet on the other hand, the choice between Lallans
and English involves a great deal of heart-searching and
probably a great deal of experimentation, and deciding to
use only the one and to drop the other is almost as
hazardous a solution as deciding to keep on using both.[7]

~~At the same time a~~ Secondly in reaction ~~to~~ against the desire of their country-

men to emulate the English ~~led~~ many thoughtful Scots in the

early years of the eighteenth century were led to a reassertion of

Scottish nationalism, ~~again~~ remarkably similar to the

assertio

[A]t the very moment when Scotland lost her political
identity that strange movement of the spirit was beginning
which was to awaken a new enthusiasm for the old songs and
the old poems and ballads, and to cause to spring once more
like a river of water in a dry place the stream of Scottish
poetry which seemed to have dried up in the arid wastes of
the seventeenth century, but which actually had only been
driven underground.8

But the interest in traditional Scottish poetry in the

beginning of the eighteenth century was not great; indeed

it was as slight as the interest taken in mid-twentieth

century in the Lallans poetry of men like Sidney Goodsir

Smith, R. Crombie Saunders and Tom Scot, to name only three

of the poets who today use the Doric, which James Thomson

was pleased to have left behind him when he "carried south

of the Border a fashion that was to produce Wordsworth."9

It was not obvious until many years after the date,

that 1706 was a milestone in Scottish literary history. In

that year James Watson, a printer at Craig's Close, Edin-

burgh, and publisher of the Edinburgh Gazette and the Edin-

burgh Courant, issued from his modest press a book which

was destined to be important in Scottish poetical litera-

ture, A Choice Collection of Comic and Serious Scots Poems

both Ancient and Modern, By Several Hands. This is the

volume which inaugurated the revival of Scots vernacular

poetry, and broke the soil in preparation for the growth of

romantic

Oxford in 1691 a transcription of <u>Christis Kirk on the Grene</u>, for which, according to W... Ker, he "ought to be honoured in Scotland as a founder of modern Scottish poetry and one of the ancestors of Burns."[10] But doubtless Professor Ker did not mean to be taken literally. Watson printed <u>Christis Kirk on the Grene</u>, along with many more Scots poems, and later Allan Ramsay transcribed it, with additions, "and, thus," said Professor Ker, more seriously, "E.C.'s new-year diversion (intended, she says, for the Saturnalia) is related to the whole movement of the age in favour of ballads and popular songs, as well as specially to the new Scottish poetry of Ramsay, Fergusson and Burns."[11]

Watson presented his first volume with an explanation and an apology:

As the frequency of Publishing Collections of Miscellaneous Poems in our neighbouring Kingdoms and States, may in a great Measure justify an Undertaking of this kind with us; so 'tis hoped that this being the first of its Nature which has been published in our Native <u>Scots</u> Dialect, the Candid Reader may be the more easily induced, through the Consideration thereof, to give some Charitable Grains of Allowance, if the Performance come not up to such a Point of Exactness as may please an over-nice Palate.[12]

He did not, however, deprecate the fact that the poems were in the vernacular. Thirty years elapsed before Scotticisms came to be regarded as downright vulgarisms; and before David Hume obliged his readers with lists of expressions to be shunned, and ninety years before James Beattie wrote of his son:

18

He as early warned against the use of Scotch words and other similar improprieties; and his dislike to them was such, that he soon learned to avoid them; and, after he grew up, could never endure to read what was written in any of the vulgar dialects of Scotland.[13]

Watson, on the other hand, apologized for his lack of competence in the Scottish dialect, a lack which Lord Hailes is later to regret in Allan Ramsay.[14] Watson's incompetence in dialect, however, (he supplied a glossary) is less disappointing to modern readers than the fact that his three volumes contain so few specimens of traditional ballad poetry. The volume of 1711 gave the earliest existing version in print of "Lady Anne Bothwell's Balow". This poem appeared in The Choice Collection as a poem of thirteen stanzas, only two of which had previously been found in print. The great importance of Watson's collection lies in the fact that it was first in the revival:

[I]t reached back over the gap of the seventeenth century to the great traditions of Scottish poetry, caught up the broken threads, and made it possible for the work to be carried on from where the Makers had left it. It did this in two ways, by making available once more specimens of the older Scottish poetry, and by collecting and preserving the stray popular poems which alone had preserved the Scottish poetic tradition throughout the seventeenth century.[15]

For a decade Watson's volumes remained the isolated source of this kind of Scottish poetry. It is difficult to gauge his influence. He symbolised the reaction to this simplification which T.S. Eliot discusses in "The Broken World", when he comments on "the alternating and periodic movents

in English literature. One is towards elaboration, the
other a reaction towards simplific tion."[16] But none
followed Watson's example until Allan Ramsay began to publish his little songs in 1720.

A digression must be made here on the subject of
ballads in England at the time of 'atson's publication. A
wider, if no more sophisticated audience than either Vatson
or Ramsay commanded, was in 1711 reading the elegant and
often wise pronouncements of Addison. Nowhere more clearly
than in his essays on ballads did Addison's far-sighted
awareness of literary currents exhibit itself, nor his
acumen in collecting ideas and testing them by his own
subtle intellect. He was not often original, and his thinking was indeed sometimes faint, but on the subject of
ballads it was unconventional and bold. His critical
theories resembled those of many earlier critics--poetry
must instruct and delight. When he decided that "Chevy
Chase" did this admirably his viewpoint was that of Sidney.
In praising the style of the ballad and analysing his
pleasure in this kind of poetry, however, he used the
critical terms of the neo-classicists. He believed the
simplicity he admired was the simplicity of art, the art
that imitated nature by noble effects, truly classical and
not "Gothick", a term he used to describe the false wit of
the meta

20

I know nothing which more shews the essential and inherent
Perfection of Simplicity of Thought, above that hich I
call the Gothick Manner in riting, than this, that the
first pleases all Kinds of Palates, and the latter only
such as have formed to themselves a wrong artificial Taste
upon little fanciful Authors and Writers of Epigram.
Homer, Virgil, or Milton, so far as the Language of their
Poems is understood, will please a Reader of plain common
Sense, who would neither relish nor comprehend an Epigram
of Martial or a Poem of Cowley: So, on the contrary, an
ordinary Song or Ballad that is the Delight of the common
People, cannot fail to please all such Readers as are not
unqualified for the Entertainment by their Affectation or
Ignorance; and the Reason is plain, because the same Paint-
ings of Nature which recommend it to the most ordinary
Reader, will appear Beautiful to the most refined.[17]

Since the version of "Chevy Chase" which Addison saw was a

very inferior variant of the ballad, it is a matter for

regret that Hearne's transcription was not available until

1719, short time after Addison's death. Durfey, in his

Pills to Purge Melancholy, 1719, used the text analysed by

Addison, and, despite Hearne's publication of a more ancient

and much superior text, the editor of Old Ballads (presumed
[18]
to be Ambrose Philips) in 1723 also used the inferior

version. Child has a note on this ballad indicating that

Addison's text should be dated not later than during the

reign of Charles the Second.

Notwithstanding the popularity of publications by

Durfey and Philips as editors, and the enthusiasm of Dorset

as a collector, Addison did not find many to share his

interest in the simple old songs. He did not escape the

scornful sarcasms of the neo-classical critics for his

regrettable lapse from good taste, nd more rea ers smiled
with Wagstaffe [19] than sighed ith Ad ison at the beauties
of "Chevy Chase". The signs of change were not yet
obvious.

But behind the front of cla sical correctness the
revolution in standards was slowly proceeding, and a clearly
recognizable contribution to the change was Allan R msay's
publishing and popularizing of Scottish b llads, beginning
in 1723, although the importance of this contribution has
not always been fully a preci ted. Burns Martin and J.W.
Oliver are at present engaged in compiling a complete edition
of his works, of which they have published two volumes of
the projected four, the t o consisting solely of the works
of Ramsay, with little in the way of biography or evalua-
tion. Perhaps when this is completed the situation will be
remedied. As Andrew Gibson pointed out in his New Light on
Allan Ramsay in 1927, biographers of the poet have been
singularly careless with facts. George Chalmers' essay in
his edition of Ramsay's poems, 1800, still remains the best
source for directly-acquired information of an essential
nature, although both Chalmers and Lord Woodhouselee, who
contributed a laudatory essay to the same volume, made
imprecise statements as to the kind of poems Ramsay first
published and the methods by which they were sold. For
example, _   ls

early poems on "single sheets of a quarto and octavo", and
Chalmers observed that these were hawked about the streets,
"and the women of Edinburgh were wont to send their children,
with a penny, to 'buy Ramsay's last piece'".[20]   These statements have been repeated by writers for the last hundred
years, but according to Gibson's careful analysis of much
evidence, "not one of those writers has furnished proof of
any kind that Ramsay published even one of his detached
pieces prior to 1721 in the form of a broadsile."[21]

   There is, however, in the Bodleian Library a small
collection of chapbooks in one binding, with the legend
"Scots Songs by Allan Ramsay, Edinburgh: Printed for the
Author at the Mercury, opposite to Niddry's Wynd, 1720."
Gibson mentions two others, issued in 1718 and 1719
respectively, and tabulates their contents. These volumes,
however, I have been unable to trace. A year later Thomas
Ruddiman published Scots Songs in a dignified quarto, with
continuous pagination, and in the same year an octavo edition
was published, with the title Poems. In all of these, however, there is only one song which has been classed as a
ballad, "Bessy Bell and Mary Gray"; and this is so much more
Ramsay than traditional ballad that it is not worthy of
inclusion in the ballad canon. Ramsay grafted an entire
new, and negligible, song on to a few lines of an old ballad,
the whole

reprinted at least thirty times in the eighteenth century,
without acquiring beauty at any printing; and in the nineteenth century Child accepted a version of it as a ballad,
though Grundtvig excluded it from the ballad c non. Child
has notes on this ballad which make it clear th t he had
not seen Ramsay's earliest printings. He has also made a
slight error concerning its text. [22]   It is a matter of
interest that the song does not appear in David Herd's first
collection, in 1769, but is printed in the editions of 1776
and 1791.

 Ramsay's special qualities are made clear in Lord
Woodhouselee's essay:

A Scotsman, in the age of Ramsay, generally rote in
English; that is, he imitated the style of the English
writers; but when he spoke, he used the langu ge of his
country. The sole peculiarity of the style of Ramsay is,
that he transferred the oral language to his writings . . . .
[H]e preferred it, as judging . . . th t it conferred a
kind of Doric simplicity.[23]

He not only transferred the oral language to the printed
page, he captured in writing some of the ballads hitherto
preserved only in oral tradition. J." Oliver in "The
Eighteenth-Century Revival", in 1933, did not minimize
Ramsay's influence:

'I knew a very wise man', wrote Fletcher of Saltoun, 'that
believed if a man were permitted to make all the ballads,
he need not care who should make the laws of a nation.'
And now when the Union, which Fletcher had opposed so
bitterly, was an accomplished fact, and Scotland had lost
the power of making her laws atson and Rams y g ve her
back her .

atson's Collection. He referred to it in 1719 in his
Familiar Epistles between Lieutenant William Hamilton
and Allan Ramsay, when he speaks of "Bonny Heck", the
famous greyhound of Hamilton's poem, which had first
appeared in Watson:

> When I begoud first to cun Verse,
> And cou'd your Ardry Whins rehearse,
> Where Bonny Heck ran fast and fierce,
>   It warm'd my Breast;
> Then Emulation did me pierce,
>   Whilk since ne'er ceast.

Nor is there evidence as to the date when he first had
access to the Bannatyne manuscript. David Irving, author
of The History of Scottish Poetry, gave the following
account of the matter:

The manuscript bears the name of "Jacobus Foulis, 1623";
and this possessor is supposed to have been Sir James
Foulis of Colinton, whose uncle George Foulis of Ravelston,
married Janet Bannatyne in the year 1601. In 1712, it was
presented by Sir William Foulis to the Hon. William
Carmichael, whose relation, the Earl of Hyndford, deposited
it in the Advocates' Library in 1772. By Mr. Carmichael
it was communicated to Allan Ramsay; who derived from it a
large proportion of his materials for the two volumes
published under the title of his Ever-Green.[25]

Irving's use of the word "communicated" is ambiguous, but

we have Ramsay's own statement:

I cannot finish this Preface, without grateful acknowledge-
ments to the Honourable Mr. William Carmichael of Skirling,
Brother to the Earl of Hyndford, who with an easy Beneficence,
that is inseparable from a superior Mind, assisted me in
this Undertaking with a valuable Number of Poems, in a
large Manuscript book in Folio, collected and wrote by Mr.
George   of the

following are gathered: and if they prove acceptable to the World, they may have the Pleasure of expecting a great many more, and shall very soon be gratified.[26]

While Ramsay was thus preparing to give what he called "valuable Remains" to "the World", a poem appeared in Edinburgh which caused excitement then, and has stirred up controversy since. Gummere calls "Hardyknute"[27] "that famous forgery . . . of Lady Wardlaw" when he discusses ballads in the Cambridge History. It was immediately accepted as a piece of genuine traditional verse, and with embellishments, or omissions, has since been included in most ballad collections. Four years later the first two volumes of A Collection of Old Ballads were published in London, and a third was issued in 1725. This was the first collection of English ballads to be printed and is of great historical interest, although compiled chiefly from seventeenth-century and contemporary broadsides. Important in ballad history is the fact that the editor collated a few of the ballads with texts found in earlier editions. The editor's point of view in the preface to a new edition published in 1726 reflects contemporary opinion:

There are many who perhaps will think it ridiculous enough to enter seriously into a Dissertation upon Ballads: and therefore I shall say as little upon the Subject as possibly I can; but I believe, it would be no difficult Matter to prove, that our Old Songs, especially those which we may properly call Historical, are written by the greatest and most polite Wits of their Age. There are many of 'em, in which we cannot possibly find a fault: Their Language is

the purest that was used in their Days, purer than was used by several great writers after their Time.[28]

In 1723, then, when Ramsay published what is believed to be the first edition of his Tea-Table Miscellany, or, Allan Ramsay's Collection of Scots Sangs, he had the field virtually to himself as far as Scots ballads were concerned. He was assiduous in his enterprises and diligent in his efforts to make the old songs of his country known. We know that he continued for several years to collect and publish almost forgotten songs and ballads in subsequent volumes of the Tea-Table, but it is difficult to get exact information as to when the earliest volumes were issued. The catalogue of an exhibition of eighteenth-century Scottish books, held in Edinburgh in 1951 states:

The first three volumes of the Tea-Table Miscellany originally came out in 1724, 1726 and 1727 respectively; of the first volume only one copy is known to exist, and of the second and third, no copies are known at all.[29]

But since the publication of the catalogue it has been made known that a volume dated 1723 is in the Sterling Memorial Library of Yale University. The volume dated 1724 is in the Huntington Library at San Marino in California. Three parts in one, numbered Volume I, dated 1727, Volume II, dated 1726, and Volume III, dated 1727, belong to Lord Haddington. A photostat of

A further difficulty in ascertaining dates of publication
presents itself in ~~the~~ Ramsay's preface already mentioned:

From this and the following volume, Mr. Thomson(who is
allowed by all, to be a good Teacher and Singer of Scots
Songs) cull'd his Orpheus Caledonius . . . . This by the
I thoughtproper to intimate, and do myself that Justice
which the publisher neglected; since he ought to have
acquainted his Illustrious List of Subscribers, that the
most of the Songs were mine, the Musick abstracted.[31]

More perplexity arises when Thomson's Orpheus Caledonius

is examined. It does contain the songs mentioned, with th

very slight differences in spelling which one expects to

find in a work of that time; but the volume is undated, an

the Bodleian Catalogue gives the date as 1725. If this da

is correct, and it would seem so, the explanation may be

that Thomson saw Ramsay's text in manuscript form. Or, as

the preface indicates,it is probable that there were earli

editions of Ramsay's work, of which no copy is at present

known.   With the increasing interest being shown in

Scottish antiquities, however,it is possible that copies

may come to light at any time. J.C. Dick in his Songs of

Robert Burns spoke of a "second edition", and gave the dat

as "1724 or 1725". I have not been able to trace any such

volume. In his bibliography Child lists the Tea-Table,

dated 1724, in four volumes, which listing further compli-

cates the situation.   Information on this matter, and

One is on no safer ground with the edition of 1730,
which was printed in London by J. Watson, and called "The
fifth edition", which Dick suggests was "a presumably un-
authorized edition". But in 1740 an edition was published
of four parts in one, in London, by A. Millar, with the
title changed to The Tea-Table Miscellany: or, A Collection
of Choice Songs, Scots and English. The simplicity of
"Scots Sangs" has been elaborated. The title page has "The
tenth edition, being the completest and most correct of any
yet published." It contains fourteen poems classified by
Child as ballads. In 1782 an edition was published which
was described as "the eighteenth".

     In 1724, however, a few months after the publication
of Tea-Table, Ramsay had brought out another miscellany,
which he called The EverGreen, being a Collection of Scots
Poems, wrote by the ingenious before 1600. This little
volume contained five ballads, among them "Johnie Armstrang"
which Ramsay stated in a footnote had never been printed
before. Three years later this poem was reprinted both in
A Collection of Old Ballads and in The Third Part of
Miscellany Poems, 1727, the latter being the fifth edition
of Dryden's Miscellany Poems. In his dedication to the
Ever Green, Ramsay, by contrast a much more acute critic
than the author of the preface to A Collection of Old
Ballads.   s .   ised

29

Everyone who has Generosity, and is not byassed with a mistaken Prejudice, will allow, th t good Sense, sharp Satyre, and witty Mirth, may be express'd with a true spirit, altho' in antiquated Words and Phrases.

J.W. Oliver says that Ramsay "spoke with a challenge to his time and to our own."[32]   How far ^he was ahead of his own time can be seen in Ramsay's preface:

I have observed that Readers of the best and most exquisite Discernment frequently complain of our modern Writings, as filled with affected Delicacies and studied Refinements, which they would gladly exchange for that natural Strength of Thought and Simplicity of Stile our Forefathers practised: To such, I hope, the following Collection of Poems will not be displeasing.
　　　When these good old Bards rote, we had not yet made Use of imported Trimming upon our Cloaths, nor of Foreign Embroidery in our Writings. Their Poetry is the Product of their own Country, not pilfered and spoiled in the Transportation from abroad: Their Images are native, and their Landskips domestick; copied from those Fields and Meadows we every Day behold.
　　　The Morning rises (in the Poets Description) as she does in the Scottish Horizon. We are not carried to Greece or Italy for a Shade, a Stream or a Breeze. The Groves rise in our own Valleys; the Rivers flow from our own Fountains, and the Winds blow upon our own Hills . . . .
　　　I hope also the Reader, when he dips into these Poems, will not be displeased with this Reflection, That he is stepping back into the Times that are past, and that exist no more. Thus the Manners and Customs then in Vogue, as he will find them here described, will have all the Air and Charm of Novelty; and that seldom fails of exciting Attention and pleasing the Mind. Besides, the Numbers, in which these Images are conveyed, will appear new and amusing.

Ramsay said he expected "Approbation and Applause", but he anticipated also "Censure and Blame". "Every Clown," he said later in the same preface, "can see that the Furrow is crooked, but where is the Man that will plow me/ one straight?"

　　　The praise followed fast, and also a measure of

blame, bt   1

showed how straight a furrow mig t be ploughed. Ramsay's

collections were popular, as the numerous editions of his

works show, but as the century ended he was criticied for

his editorial policies, or for lack of them. Chalmers, in

his biography of Ramsay, admitted the blame while qualifying

it: "It seems to be universally agreed that Ramsay failed

in this difficult undertaking."[33]   Irving's criticism in

1861 damned with faint praise:

It was his original intention to prepare one or two volumes
more, but no sequel ever made its appearance, nor can it
excite much regret that the editor should have failed to
perform his promise; his extreme licentiousness in adding
or retrenching according to his own fancy, amounted to a
complete disqualification for such an undertaking. His
publication, however, was not without its utility; it
tended in a considerable degree to revive among his country-
men a taste for vernacular poetry, and to direct the
attention of the more learned antiquaries to Bannatyne's
precious collection.[34]

Millar, in his Literary History of Scotland, 1903, showed

the influence of his time less, and was somewhat more

generous in his estimate:

[Ramsay] set himself, with the assistance of certain
"ingenious young gentlemen" to provide sets of verses,
modelled more or less closely upon those handed down by
tradition, which should not be unworthy of the irs with
which they were to be conjoined. The "ingenuity" of the
editor and his subordinates may sometimes h ve been mis-
placed, and their zeal may have outrun discretion; but it
cannot be doubted that Ramsay has preserved for us much
that might otherwise have been irrevocably lost. And what
is particularly noticeable in him is his fearle s and
confident assertion of the claims of the national muse.[35]

Unfortunately Ramsay brought to light no more

ballads a   t   _ _ _   _   _ ___ __ _

published in London from the press of A. Moore, called *A New Miscellany of Scots Songs*, and contained six ballads already found in the *Tea-Table*. The volume was anonymous, though Ramsay's portrait opposite the title page was hardly consonant with anonymity. Four of these ballads were transcribed in *A Collection of Old Ballads* in 1738. A new edition of the *Ever Green* appeared in 1761, and in 1770, *Thirty Scots Songs*, which included six ballads already printed, was published, with "Allen Ramsey" [sic] on the title page. By adding these publications to the various editions of the *Tea-Table*, and remembering that Percy did not publish the *Reliques* until 1765, we realize that for forty years the publications of Ramsay were responsible for keeping the Scots popular ballad before the public.

During these forty years the interest in ballad poetry was steadily increasing. Thomas and Joseph Warton, Shenstone, Gray and others of lesser literary importance were all attracted by ballads, as their letters and works show. Even Johnson showed considerable interest in the topic, although he must be included here with reservations. However no attempt was made between the date of Ramsay's collections and Percy's *Reliques* to assemble into book

the field of ballad collecting, with its importance in the
romantic revival, the part played by Ramsay in this aspect
of romanticism has been, until very recently, unduly
minimized, if not, indeed, as in the case of Burns Martin's
biography of Ramsay, denied existence. Even Hans Hecht,
strangely enough, did not accord him justice here:

The honour of having revived English and Scottish popular
poetry remains for ever and unreservedly with Thomas Percy,
Robert Burns and Walter Scott, whose knowledge and art lent
adequate expression to the vivid emotions of the time.[36]

Ramsay's conscientious biographer, George Chalmers, placed
him with "the almost forgotten poets of Scotland", but
equally just is the estimate of his position made by
Margaret Sherwood in Undercurrents of Influence in English
Romantic Poetry:

Deeply significant was the recognition, coming earlier in
England than in Germany, of the values of folk poetry;
Ramsay in the heart of the psuedo-classic period had been a
pioneer in this matter.[37]

He must be accorded his place, minor though it may be, among
the original explorers, in the list begun in the sixth
century by another writer also born north of the Tweed,
Gildas of Ailclyd, the earliest of British historians, of
whom Agnes Mure Mackenzie observes:

The oldest extant piece of literature known to have been
produced by a man of these islands is the work of a sixth-
century monk of Dumbarton. It is not without significance,
perhaps, that this senior work of all Scottish, and British,
letters, is a tale of disaster, of the shattering of a
culture that seemed immortal . . .[38]

n the ver Green, an there is no rea n to

the

say was res onsible for t e polishin an /s

ts which make these two poems outs anding a

tional ballads. In his orres ond nce of

alrymple, or alies, alconer praises him

l discrimination in selection he di ot lac

ill always belon the credit of avin led t

timulating others who were better sc olars .

Since the writer's views on amsay as a pre-

differ from those of urns rtin, most re

of the poet, it may be well to lo k briefly

y. rofessor artin wishes "to evaluate his

admirable goal of dispassionate writing, which he set himself.[41]

    Nor was Martin on stable ground when he stated that
the bulk of Ramsay's work shows him to have been especially
sympathetic towards neo-classicism. No man can write
completely out of his time, and the climate of opinion in
which Ramsay worked was early eighteenth-century neo-
classic, as the wholly delightful preface to his Ever Green
so clearly shows. Here certainly was poetic diction and an
aesthetic judgment couched in Addison's own tones. But
there was more than that. And Martin -- was it unwittingly?
-- stated what this was:

Ramsay's aim was not to produce a scholarly text but, at a
time when poetry was just reviving in Scotland and was in
great danger of turning wholly to English models, to arouse
interest in the older vernacular poetry -- partly for
literary reasons, but mainly, so it seems to the present
writer, for national and patriotic reasons.[42]

But is it necessarily nationalism to describe a Scottish
background, or patriotism to go back to "that natural
Strength of Thought and Simplicity of Stile our Forefathers
practised"? I suggest that Ramsay's interest in "the Times
that are past, and that exist no more" was not merely the
interest of an antiquarian, but also of a man of sensibility
and some aesthetic discernment. In an essay on Thomas Gray,
Lord David Cecil observed:

Why the
century   the

sober rationalism which permeated the general outlook of
the age, led its more poetic spirits to find contemporary
life intolerably prosaic. Their imagination felt constrict-
ed by the spectacle of the world of their own time. They
therefore sought relief by escaping mentally to the
contemplation of other and less rational periods.[43]

But only a romantic seeks relief in the past, and I believe

that it was Ramsay's romanticism mainly which led to his

"interest in the older vernacular poetry", whereas his

national and patriotic fervour spurred him in the direction

of purely Scottish literature.

That Ramsay was fortunate in his heritage, none ill

deny. As William Beattie remarks:

[S]een against a wide background of poetic revivals and
developments the English ballads are crude and wooden, whereas the Scottish, uncertain and commonplace though they can
often be, yet rise out of that level into a poetic and
dramatic intensity that remains their secret.[44]

Scottish ballads had not been vitiated by the printers of

broadsides and stall copies, as had English ballads, (see

Appendix B), and to Scotland also must go the honour of
[45]
printing for the first time three ballads vastly different

from those complained about in contemporary publications.

Since chapbooks were usually produced as cheaply as possible,

they were seldom distinguished either by their typography

or accuracy of text. But the work of Robert and Andrew
[46]
Foulis, printers to the Glasgow University from 1742

until their deaths, is a great exception; their chapbooks

are note

textual accuracy of material. Since today the rare copies
of their chapbooks extant are generally encountered bound
with others of the period, a cursory glance will show the
superiority of the Foulis brothers' work. That chapbooks
have survived at all is surprising, since these insubstantial
booklets were originally issued unbound, or in flimsy
wrappers. We are indeed fortunate that all of the ballads
to come from the Foulis Press have survived these two
hundred and twenty years.[47] It will be made clear when
"Edom o Gordon" is collated that the Foulis Brothers did
not follow Ramsay's example and "improve" the poems in the
printing. It is equally obvious that they manifested no
critical sense in classifying their material: the much
inferior "Two old historical Scots Poems" are given the
same treatment as the three fine ballads, and issued without editorial comment; a procedure shortly to be followed by
the great Scottish ballad collector, David Herd. But four
years before Herd published his first collection, the pre-
dominance of Scottish interest in ballad poetry was
challenged by the most enthusiastic ballad collector of the
period, the English Thomas Percy.

Chapter three

THE GREAT COLLECTORS: PERCY, HERD AND RITSON

The assigning of specific dates to a literary age is
often misleading. It may impose arbitrary limits not only
undesirable, but inaccurate. The most I wish to do in this
chapter is to indicate some of the signs that point to the
third quarter of the eighteenth century as the centre of
the transition period between the classical age, characterized by what Cazamian calls its "lucid self-mastery", and
the romantic age with its rich self-expression; and to
consider, both from a historial and a critical point of
view, the part played in the transition by Thomas Percy,
David Herd and Joseph Ritson, the three most important
ballad collectors to arise in the second half of the
century.

One of the important signs of the transition was
the interest taken in translations from poetry of writers
remote in time, place and spirit. Ker has shown the
importance of Temple's essay, "Of Heroic Virtue", where
Temple "notices the song of Ragnar because it explains
something of the past, and contributes something to the
1
experien   .   y,

"Of Poetry", Temple "takes up 'runic' literature";[2] but his remained a more or less isolated voice until Gray observed in "The Progress of Poesy", 1754, that it was possible to find the poetic muse in the untutored verses of Laplanders and South American Indians; and Macpherson in 1760 began to publish the Ossianic poems which, "whatever one may think of them now, exercised a European influence, making Scotland, in the eyes of the world, the true and only home of Romance."[3]

To read today Macpherson's "Dissertation concerning the Poems of Ossian", and Hugh Blair's "Critical Dissertation on the Poems of Ossian" is a valuable aid to understanding the literary climate which produced the great ballad collectors, particularly Percy and his circle, the climate wherein two widely disparate beliefs were held at the same time. Ossian is an epic poem, classical in effect, which the author and his admirers astonishingly affirmed was simpler than Homer, as full of sensibility as Virgil. Nevertheless in his dissertation Macpherson set down his ideas:

The nobler passions of the mind never shoot forth more free and unrestrained than in the times we call barbarous. That irregular manner of life, and those manly pursuits, from which barbarity takes its name, are highly favourable to a strength of mind unknown in polished times . . . . The human passions lie in some degree concealed behind forms and artificial manners; and the powers of the soul, without an opportunity of exerting them, lose their vigour.[4]

Blair advanced to his argument through a discussion of the way in which the understanding gains ground over the imagination: "Hence poetry, which is the child of imagination, is frequently most glowing and animated in the first ages of society."[5] As an example of untamed imagination he turned back to the illustration used by Temple, "The Death Song of Ragnar", as preserved by Olaus Vormius, which he transcribed and commented upon:

This is such poetry as we might expect from a barbarous nation. It breathes a most ferocious spirit. It is will, harsh, and irregular; but at the same time animated and strong; the style, in the original, full of inversions, and, as we learn from some of Olaus's notes, highly metaphorical and figured.[6]

But a poem of this kind could not commend itself wholeheartedly to one steeped in the sensibility of the age, and it is not surprising to find that Blair wrote:

But when we open the works of Ossian, a very different scene presents itself. There we find the fire and enthusiasm of the most early times, combined with an amazing degree of regularity and art. We find tenderness, and even delicacy of sentiment, greatly predominant over fierceness and barbarity. Our hearts are melted with the softest feelings, and at the same time elevated with the highest ideas of magnanimity, generosity and true heroism. When we turn from the poetry of Lodbrog to that of Ossian, it is like passing from a savage desert into a fertile and cultivated country.[7]

Ossian has a "Solemn and awful grandeur", and

[I]n point of humanity, magnanimity, virtuous feelings of every kind . . . not only the heroes of Homer, but even those of the polite and refined Virgil, are left far behind by those of Ossian.[8]

Although the reaction from the artificiality of the classical

age was not yet well-established, the transition was in progress. "The public h s seen all th t art can do," wrote William Shenstone to John MacGowan in 1761, "and they want the more striking efforts of wild, original, enthusiastic genius."[9] In view of Shenstone's work at this time in pruning the ballads to make them suitable for men of taste, this statement is typical of the inconsistencies of the age.

The "more learned antiquaries" who succeeded Ramsay, did not confine their interest only to Gaelic, Norse, Iselandic [sic] and Welsh. They began to turn their attention to the neglected treasures of their own language. After publishing his "Five Pieces of Runic Poetry", Percy borrowed from Allen Ramsay's son the transcripts of David Lyndsay's Interludes, which Ramsay had begun in 1724 and had returned to after twenty years.[10]

I do not wish to over simplify here; to maintain that all writers and scholars in Britain were interested in antiquities in general and ballads in particular. It is nevertheless true that the vivid emotions of the time called for adequate expression, and this could not always be found in the "order" and "reason" of the neo-classical poets. Readers were no longer satisfied with a composition wherein one "might suppose that the poem was written for a wager, to prove that country life might be described, and nothing called by its name."[11] Simplicity of diction was

sought, but fervour and passion must accompany the simplicity. The primitivism which had spre d to nature in both philosophy and gardening, was, as Lovejoy pointed out, extended to literature.[12]   The necessary qualities were not to be found in the contempor ry poetry of a literate people. But they were found in ballads.

Among the distinguishing features of ballad poetry are its vocabulary, rhetoric and complete freedom from fashionable poetic diction. The "wan water" and the "lily lee", "the black steed or the brown" belong to no period -- they are ballad epithets. But also peculiar to this kind of poetry is the point of view found in a ballad, a point of view which is direct, simple, primitive. Love, sex, jealousy, violence, superstition and death are all presented with a matter-of-fact directness, uncomplicated by orthodox moralizing, although ballads have their own moral values. The result of this directness is a dramatic compression, which brings to the reader a sudden sense of different standards. As C.V. Deane has said in his <u>Aspects of Eighteenth Century Native Poetry</u>, "the ballads came to be powerful dissolvents of eighteenth-century poetic complacency".[13] In them was found the freedom from rules, and from the false wit which Addison had deplored: here was the "painting of nature" described by Joseph Warton. Deane has a paragraph on ballad phr aeology hich is pertinent at this point:

42

If their work points in many ways to a transitional state of taste, it can hardly be said that the eighteenth-century ballad editors were conscious of preparing the way for a grand revolution in poetic aims. They did not hold that the taste for the polished verse of their contemporaries was likely to be dispelled by the appeal of these more roughly-moulded treasures of the past. It does not seem unjustifiable to suppose, therefore, that their evident appreciation of the formal elements in the oral poetry -- or, as Percy put it, 'a cast of style and measure very different from that of contemporary poets of a higher class; and many phrases and idioms, which the minstrels seem to have appropriated to themselves' -- may have been quickened by the fact that an equally conventional phraseology was prevalent in the verse of their own age.[14]

On to the stage then, thus adequately furnished, in 1765, and with a receptive audience already assembled, came treading delicately, but firmly, Thomas Percy. Percy was a man of his time. Few can regret that it fell to his lot to rescue the old folio MS. from Humphrey Pitt's housemaid. Hecht, whose assessment of Percy's contribution has already been noted, praised his "knowledge and art". Professor Clawson in his article, Percy's Reliques of Ancient English Poetry, showed how susceptible Percy was to the literary currents and tendencies of his age, while attributing to him more originality than is generally accorded today:

His literary ambitions, facile pen, assimilative and sympathetic power of appreciating and reflecting what he read, delicate but somewhat narrow literary judgment, and slender but genuine poetic talent made him capable of presenting this popular material in a form which would arrest public attention.[15]

That Percy appreciated the "poetry in a state of nature" which he found in the folio, is beyond doubt, and his desire

to share it was genuine; but equally strong is his anxiety
to conform to the standards of contemporary correctness.
Here was the conflict already evident in the assertion
of Macpherson and, later, of Blair. Despite his real
enthusiasm for his subject Percy felt the need to apologise
for the collection he offered to the public. True, Watson
and Ramsay had both prefaced their collections with
deferential explanations; but these men had been pioneers,
and the time not ripe for their kind of offering. Percy,
on the other hand, published his selections from the folio
MS. not only with the blessing of "the author of the
'Rambler' and the late Mr. Shenstone", but indeed on the
"importunity of several learned and ingenious friends".[16]
The preface to the first edition of the _Reliques_[17] shows
how fortunately situated Percy was to undertake his chosen
task. Watson had been a busy printer, Ramsay a wig-maker,
but Percy was a scholar and a gentleman. As chaplain to
the Earl of Sussex he had means and some leisure; as a man
he had a lively curiosity, and as a literary connoisseur he
had scholarly friends who were all ardent admirers of this
"new, irregular poetry". He was even able to protest that
"To the friendship of Dr. Samuel Johnson he owes many hints
for the conduct of the work". Despite the assistance of
scholars who supplied him with manuscripts and annotations,
Percy cautiously says that "he was long in doubt whether,

in the present state of improved literature, they [the ballads] could be deemed worthy the attention of the public."[18]   That his admission was not naiveté becomes evident from an examination of some of his voluminous correspondence.

An adequate estimate of Percy's position in the world of letters of the second half of the eighteenth century has not yet been made, although as Watkin-Jones pointed out thirty years ago:

It seems that a thorough biography is necessary to do justice to a man of so many activities. Such a biography would also do inestimable service as a guidebook or map to this abundant period, revealing much information about the literary and social activities of the time.[19]

Realization of the fundamental importance in literary history of an inquiry into the diaries and vast correspondence left by Percy, who, having a sound idea as to its value caused much of it to be collected during his lifetime, has led David Nichol Smith and Cleanth Brooks, as general editors, to publish some of this fund of material; though much MS. material remains untouched as yet.[20]

It is an anomaly that the very qualities for which Professor Clawson praised Percy are those which damned him in the eyes of his contemporary, Joseph Ritson, critical student, historian and antiquarian, but only occasionally a man of taste. Percy was at all times willing to sacrifice accuracy and fidelity on the altar of good taste as he

understood it. He was frank about t is characteristic, nd hardly found it a defect. An indefati ble worker, he carefully colleted transcri ts with their ori inals, and spared no pains to pick u information. owe er, "to edit" meant "to improve", and the notion of "i proving" or "refining" the ballads was a constant subject of is correspondence. nd if r. Johnson pontificated that t e "reading of ancient books is probably true, nd is t ere-fore not to be disturbed for t e sake of ele ance, perspicuity, or mere improvement of the sense"[21], ercy gave no si n that he heard. He believed himself to be not only sufficiently honest in is editing, but deservin of praise for is methods, and even for is disarming, if mistaken, modesty in the preface:

[W]hen, by a few slight correct ons or addit o s, most beautiful or interesting sense hath started forth . . . the ditor could seldom prevail on hi self to indulge the vanity of aking a formal clai to the improvement; ut must plead guilty to the charge of concealing his own share in the amendments under som such eneral title as a odern Copy," or the like . . . . his object was to please both the judicious anti uary and the reader of taste; and he hath endeavoured to gratify both wit out offending either.

Until the publication of the ercy- enstone correspondence by ans echt, the reasons for the individual amendments were a mat er for conjecture, alt ou h the publication of the Folio anuscript by ales and Fur ivall in 1867 enabled Child to set down a comparison of the . texts with t ose

.

of Percy, taken, as he said, from the folio, a task not
possible for the early editors, who had not been permitted
a glimpse of the folio. The Percy-Shenstone correspondence,first
edited by Hecht, shows Percy's mind at work. For example,
in November 1757, some months after the production in
London of John Home's _Douglas,_ the tragedy founded on "Gil
Morice", Percy wrote to Shenstone to tell him that he had
a MS. version of "Gil Morice" which Johnson urged him to
publish, although Boswell reported of _Douglas_ that Johnson
had said angrily that there were not "ten good lines in
the whole play".[22] Two months later Shenstone wrote back
quoting stanzas of the same ballad, which he believed were
an improvement on those in Percy's copy:

> His hair was like the threeds of gold
> Shot frae the burning sun,
> His lips like roses dropping dew,
> His breath was a perfume.[23]

Shenstone's version is oddly reminiscent of lines in a
short poem by an anonymous author which appeared in _The
Edinburgh Miscellany,_ 1720, wherein a lady's hair is described as: "Of shining Threed, shot from the Sun,/ And
twisted into line."[24] Percy expressed his gratitude for
Shenstone's help, finding that the versions "differ in a
surprising manner; scarcely two lines are found alike".[25]
The ballad remained uppermost in his mind. Again he wrote:

I can think of no rhyme for Sun in the 14th Stanza of the
additions to Gil Morrice -- but what if you find one for

perfume _in. ult_. Query? Threeds of Gold drawn from
Minerva's Loom -- or something infinitely better.[26]

One need not conclude that Shenstone approved of the ver-

sion Percy finally published in the _Reliques_:

> His hair was like the threeds of gol.,
> Drawne frae Minervas loome:
> His lipps like roses dra_ing dew,
> His breath was a' perfume.

Even the simple perfume has now become "all perfume". He

had now confirmed his belief that if being Scots tended to

make a ballad good, being more Scots would make it better.

An example of superlative understatement occurred in the

notes Percy appended to this ballad:

As this Poem lays claim to a pretty high Antiquity, we
have assigned it a place among our early Pieces: though,
after all, there is reason to believe it has received very
considerable Modern Improvements.

Percy had indeed reason to believe so! This same remark

is repeated in all subsequent editions of the _Reliques_, but

with additional notes.

An early letter from Percy to Shenstone makes it

clear that the collaborators did not always agree:

By Mr. Dodsley I rec'd the favour of your Corrections of the
Rhymes you were so good as to look over: to your Pen they
are now indebted for Beauties they were not before
possess'd of. You will notwithstanding (I flatter myself)
make Allowances for the foolish Fondness of Scriblers, if
you sh'd find I have now and then ventur'd to retain the
old Reading, in Defiance of your superior Judgment.[27]

They were equally culpable, however, in their editorial

methods, and equally deserving of the scorn and censure

Joseph | yet

no formula or specific criterion for a ballad is obvious
throughout the correspondence, although Shenstone attempted
a very simple definition in a letter to Percy: "I . . . am
apt to consider a Ballad as containing some little story,
either real or invented."[28] It remained for Ritson to
differentiate clearly between song and ballad, and to make
the now accepted statement that a ballad is a lyrical
narrative.

Percy's correspondence with Scottish antiquaries,
begun in 1762, is illuminating. In January 1763 he wrote
to David Dalrymple (later Lord Hailes) suggesting the
mingling of two ballads, "Adam Carre" and "Edom O' Gordon",
in order to make "one elegant ballad". And in the same
letter he said:

Should any improvement either in Sentiment or Expression
occur, I should not scruple to insert it, provided it were
not inconsistent with the general Plan or style of the
Poem.[29]

His complacency here regarding his ability to improve the
poems is rather remarkable, considering that he was to write
to Dalrymple a few months later: "In some of the Scottish
Ballads I meet with expressions which the Glossaries I have
at hand either wholly omit, or do not explain to my satisfaction."[30] And a year later, regarding "Scottisms", he
wrote:

Mr. Johnson (Author of the 'Rambler') who has been with me
for 2 mo`` `                 `   gives

them up as inexplicable: and as he has a good deal of
Glossarizing knowledge, it will be some honour to succeed,
after he has given them over.[31]

Obviously Percy and his correspondents found nothing
reprehensible in using Procrustean methods on the old
poems. John Wotherspoon, the able printer of the collection
of ballads published in 1769 by David Herd, not only agreed
with their methods, but offered approval. Herd was the
most faithful and trustworthy editor of old songs and
ballads yet to appear on the scene. Lacking the "facile
pen" and "poetic talent" of Percy, but with far less concern
for the sensibilities of the man of taste or feeling, Herd
succeeded in pleasing the latter, as well as the judicious
antiquary. After reading Herd's volume with pleasure,
Percy proposed through an intermediary, George Paton,
friend of contemporary Scots scholars and writers, to use
Herd's MS. in a forthcoming volume. Wotherspoon replied to
Paton:

My friend, Mr. Herd, obliged me with a sight of Dr. Percy's
letter to you respecting the Scottish Songs, &c., which I
now return. -- Be pleased to inform that gentleman, that
we chearfully consent to his making the use he proposes of
our MS. vol. by extracting such fragments as he thinks
proper to adopt into his plan. These mutilated antiques
thus perfected and restored by Dr. Percy, will give us a
pleasure resembling that which we should feel from beholding
the injuries of time on a statue of Phidias or Polycletus
repaired by the hand of Buonarruoti [sic].[32]

Today few readers would disagree with Holgart that
as "scholarship the collection [the Reliques] is useless,
and ...

concur, as would have even the redoubtable Ritson, when he
added, "it is nevertheless a remarkable achievement".[33]
The publication of the _Reliques_ resulted in a furore similar
to that caused by _Ossian_. In Britain within two years
the demand resulted in a second edition, similar to the first
but not identical with it. Ancient manuscripts were turning up; "old women and nurses" were persuaded to remember
and recite or sing other versions than those "purified"
by Percy; and the excellent chapbooks of Robert and Andrew Foulis
increasingly circulated. Sudden retribution did not fall
upon Percy, but criticisms of his first edition were not
lacking. In the second edition he found it necessary to
make changes, add explanatory notes, and sometimes modify
or amplify the notes he had already given. But these
changes did not necessarily make for improvement or more
accuracy. Sometimes Percy, like Dr. Blair, had too much
sensibility; a condition regretted by Dr. Johnson, when
he pronounced that Mrs. Percy "had more sense than her
husband".[34]

It was reasonable that Dr. Johnson should be mild
in his strictures. He had greatly encouraged Percy in
the early days of their mutual interest in ballads. Indeed Irving Churchill declares that only Johnson's preparation of his edition of Shakespeare prevented him from
being co-editor.[35] But Percy's greatest critic was not a gentleman. Today

Ritson's thunder perhaps tells us less about Percy than it
does about Ritson, although one admits that the thunder was
justifiable:

The history of Scotish poetry exhibits a series of fraud,
forgery, and imposture, practised with impunity and success.
The ballad of Gil Morrice, was rinted, for the second time,
at Glasgow, [by the brothers Foulis] in 1755, with an advertisement, setting forth "that its preservation was o..ing to
a lady, who favoured the rinters with a copy, as it was
carefully collected from the mouths of old omen and
nurses;" and "any reader that can render it more correct
or complete," is desired to oblige the public with such
improvements. In consequence of this advertisement, as e
learn from Dr. Percy, no less than sixteen additional verses
were produced and handed about in manuscript, which that
editor, though he conjectures them after all to be only an
ingenious interpolation, has inserted, in their proper
places . . . .   The doctor assures us, that in his ancient
folio MS. "is a very imperfect copy of the same ballad:
wherein, though the leading features of the story are the
same, yet the colouring here is so much improved and
heightened, and so many additional strokes are thrown in,
that it is evident the whole has undergone a revisal . . . ."
The original stanzas, even as the ballad is now printed,
may be easily distinguished from the interpolations; great
part of the latter being a[n] . . . evident and pitiful
forgery.[36]

Ritson saw no chance of being allowed to examine the folio

MS. It was easier for Hales to be amiable eighty years

later, when he and Furnivall had the precious document in

their possession:

The extent to which Percy used his Folio MS. in his Reliques
has been concealed by his misstatement, that of the pieces
he published "The greater part of them are extracted from
an ancient folio manuscript in the Editor's possession,
which contains near 200 poems, songs and "metrical romances."
        The Reliques (1st ed.) contains 176 pieces, and of
these the Folio is used only in 45; so that for Percy's
"greater part" we should read "about one-fourth", and, if his
term "extracted" is to be taken strictly, "not one-sixth".
It is perhaps too bad to follow Bp. Colenso in applying the

test of numbers to poetical statements, but the result may as well be known.[37]

Since changes and additions will be shown in chapters four and five, one illustration of Percy's technique may suffice here. The edition of 1775 followed more or less the same lines as the text of 1767, with re-touching and re-editing still the order of the day, and misleading statements set down as facts. The old Scots song "John Anderson my jo" suffered particularly reprehensible changes. It was given in the edition of 1765 as follows:

> Woman.
> John Anderson my jo, cum in as ze gae bye,
> And ze sall get a sheips heid weel taken in a pye;
> Weel baken in a pye, and the haggis in a pat;
> John Anderson my jo, cum in, and ze's get that.
>
> Man.
> And how doe ze, Cummer? and how doe ze thrive?
> And how mony bairns hae ze? Wom. Cummer, I hae five.
> Man. Are they to zour awin gude man? Wom. Na, Cummer, na;
> For four of tham were gotten, quhan Wullie was awa'.

The accompanying note explained:

It is a received tradition in Scotland that at the time of the Reformation, ridiculous and bawdy songs were composed by the rabble to the tunes of the most favourite hymns in the Latin service . . . . John Anderson my jo was [one of these].

The edition of 1767 followed that of 1765 as to text, but in the edition of 1775 the sea change occurred. The five bairns were turned into seven, and Percy appended the following:

In the present Edition this song is much improved by some new readings communicated by a friend; who thinks the

"Seven Bairns", in st. 2nd. allude to the Seven Sacraments; five of which were the spurious offs ring of Mother Church: ae [misprint for as] the first st. contains a satirical allusion to the luxury of the popish clergy.

Percy gave no authority for his changes, and he was not convincing as to the satirical allusion. Nor was there any proof for his "received tradition" with regard to the music of the song; indeed the opposite was true, and sacred words were given to the secular tunes, a fact which Ritson seized on eagerly. Too much blame however should not be attached to Percy in this case. Even William Tytler, an acknowledged authority on Scottish music, had fallen into the same error, and Ritson's wrath descended upon him also. But in this case Percy went his unrepentant way, and the notes and the bairns remained uncorrected. It is a small pleasure to add that Ritson nodded for once, and misquoted Percy, turning Percy's four bairns into three.

By the time Percy's third edition reached the public, David Herd's anonymous volume of 1769 had achieved so much favourable notice that Herd felt justified in issuing his collection rearranged and extended into two volumes, which appeared in 1776. Stern critical faculties were not yet brought to bear on ballads, but Herd e rnestly strove for accuracy, and he was not troubled over much by the delicacy of feeling admired by Percy. Considering Herd's importance in the ballad history of the eighteenth century, it is un   y

the neglect which has been his portion. Hans Hecht's Songs
from David Herd's Manuscripts, published in 1904, remains
the best available source for facts on "the most indefatig-
able and the most conscientious of the old Scots collectors".
Hecht drew largely on James Maidment's publications of the
correspondence of George Paton, Herd's friend and one of the
original members of the Society of Antiquaries of Scotland.[38]
Paton is worthy of notice; as Hecht wrote:

[H]is influence on the men of letters of his day must not be
underrated. His comprehensive knowledge equally with his
celebrated library was common property, and he imparted it
with a liberality which gained him wide influence with the
best intellect of his time . . . . The total number of his
correspondents amounts to fifty-four, amongst whom are Lord
Hailes, Thomas Percy, Joseph Ritson, David Herd, James
Cummyng, Gilbert Stuart and Lord Buchan.[39]

Hecht added his regret that no editor has undertaken to
finish the task so well begun by Maidment, but rejoiced
that such a widely-read book as Pennant's Tour in Scotland
made enthusiastic acknowledgment of Paton's unselfish and
faithful assistance to the literary undertakings of his
friends.[40]

It is clear that Herd had scant literary ambition.
His first volume, The Ancient and Modern Scots Songs,
Heroic Ballads, &c., was published anonymously. The preface
is important historically, and as giving evidence of the
trend ballad collecting had begun to follow:

The only collection upon our plan, consisting entirely of
Scots Son

number, with the music, and now b come very scarce; for
Allan Ramsay's *Tea-Table Miscellany* cannot be termed
A Complete Collection of Scots Songs; they are, as he
himself entitles them, -- *A Choice Collection of Scots and
English.*

The valuable collection of Percy has furnished
some songs, and more perfect copies of several ballads,
than those formerly printed; and when modern words could
only be given to ancient tunes, these are, however (to
speak en *Ecossois*) composed by Poets natives of North
Britain.

After the manner of Percy, it was at first intended
to have prefixed notes to the more ancient and historical
poems in this collection; but the volume would have been
thereby too much swelled; and as the Editor hath already
some prospect of materials for a second, he is of opinion
that these notes will come in with more propriety at the
conclusion where they may be by themselves perused.

In 1776 the collection was issued again, in two volumes,
with "The Second Edition" on the title page of the second
volume. The work was again anonymous, and ... Henderson
is not accurate when he says in *Scottish Vernacular
Literature* that Herd's name was given as editor of the
volumes.[41]

here were improvements, additions, modifications and
omissions in the edition of 1776. It was enthusiastically
received, and no dissenting voice appears to have been
raised save only that of John Pinkerton. The statement in
Chambers' Cyclopedia of Literature, 1903, that "Herd did
for Scottish song what Bishop Percy had done for English
Ballads" does not over-state the importance of Herd's
collections. Their influence can be clearly seen. Burns's
debt to Herd is made clear in the notes in Henley and Henderson's
Centenary Edition of Burns's Poems. Scott made no secret
of his re

well as a man. As the introduction to Border Minstrelsy

shows, Scott was indebted to Herd for much valuable material:

To the politeness and liberality of Mr. Herd, of Edinburgh,
the editor of the first classical collection of Scottish
songs and ballads,.,the editor is indebted for the use of
his MSS., containing songs and ballads, published and unpublished, to the number of ninety and upwards.

In Familiar Letters of Sir Walter Scott is a pen portrait

of Herd, composed by Scott after Herd had been dead for

fifteen years.[42] But it could be argued that years are

kind and Scott was not always discriminating. Perhaps more

critical praise came from Ritson, of whom Scott had written:

"As bitter as gall, and as sharp as a razor,"[43] but whom

even his enemies acclaimed as an acute and just critic:

To this [collection], though not so judiciously selected
or arranged as it might have been, and containing many con-
fessedly English songs, a few supposititious ballads, and
several pieces unworthy of preservation, we are certainly
indebted for a number of excellent and genuine compositions,
never before printed, as the author of the present collection is bound in gratitude to acknowledge.[44]

Ritson's indebtedness to Herd included the loan of Herd's

MS., and interesting sidelights on the characters of the two

men appear in the correspondence regarding it, which has

already been referred to.

Ritson is nowadays so much in the forefront of

ballad discussions, that his position in literature may well

be defined here. Henry Alfred Burd, who in 1915 published

Joseph Ritson, A Critical Biography, puts the case for Rit-

son into the first paragraph of his preface:

Joseph Ritson is a minor figure in the literary history of the latter half of the eighteenth century. But he was one of the chief instruments in bringing about the changes in that period of remarkable transition. Although a potent factor in reviving the interest in ballads and old poetry and in hastening the acceptance of advanced standards of editorship and criticism, he has been largely ignored in the historical appraisement of the romantic movement. This neglect was not altogether unnatural. Ritson's method of criticism was so invidiously personal and his beliefs and habits were so eccentric that attention was attracted primarily to his peculiarities, while his stable qualities were overlooked by the majority. As a consequence of the silence which early enshrouded his name, an adequate estimate of his literary place has, up to the present, been impossible.

To ap raise Ritson, as in the case of any writer, it is

best, generally, to go to the fountainhead, to the writer

himself; and for this appraisal an examination of the Percy-

Ritson controversy is illuminating. To this end a disser-

tation written by Ritson in 1783 will serve as a beginning.

Ritson was a collector of literary antiquities, and one of

his earliest publications was A Select Collection of English

Songs, to which he prefixed a dissertation entitled "A

Historical Essay on the Origin and Progress of National

Song". This was inspired directly by the essay "On the

Ancient English Minstrels", with which Percy had prefaced

his Reliques almost twenty years earlier, and which had

ap eared unchanged in two subsequent editions. Percy's

essay was designed to show that minstrels were composers,

musicians, poets and singers, quite often all four functions

being combined in one person; and as such they held an

exalted

continued to do so for hundreds of years after the Conquest.
Percy embellished his essay with the fruits of scholarship
in the form of lavish quotations, anecdotes and conjectures;
and as proof positive, he quoted a letter from an eye-
witness of an entertainment given in 1575, where one of
the entertainers was garbed as "an ancient MINSTRAL". A
note of modern verisimilitude was injected into the romantic
picture: "A pair of pumps on his feet, with cross cut at
his toes for corns: not new indeed, yet cleanly blackt with
soot, and shining as a shoing horn." The less discursive
essay accorded well with the agreeable texts and
notes of the Reliques. Pinkerton loudly admired it in
1776, repeated his admiration in 1781, and again in 1733,
just before he read Ritson. But Ritson had not been idle.
Unimpressed by either Percy's romance or his realism, and
with the fanatic zeal and painstaking labour which
characterized him in all his undertakings, Ritson, in his
"Historic Essay" refuted and ridiculed Percy's cherished
theories. His method was to give facts, not to make
generalizations, and he gathered together a store of
references, all to show that Percy was gravely misinformed.
According to Percy:

The Minstrels seem to have been the genuine successors of
the ancient Bards, who . . . sung verses to the harp, of
their own composing . . . . Our Saxon ancestors . . . had
been accustomed to hold men of their profession in the
highest reverence. Their skill was considered as something

divine, their persons were deemed sacred, their attendance
was solicited by kings, and they were everywhere loaded with
honours and rewards.

This indiscriminate use of the term "minstrel" to cover a

whole group of entertainers was summarily dismissed by Ritson

in his "Observations on the Ancient English Minstrels":

Under this comprehensive term minstrel . . . we are to include
the trouveur, or poet, the chanteur or vocal performer, and
the menêtrier, or musician; not to mention the fablier, conteur,
jugleur, baladin, &c. all which were sometimes distinct pro-
fessions, and sometimes united in one and the same man.

Ignoring the evidence Percy had amassed, Ritson declared that

Percy's statements were pure conjectures.   Like Hume, he asked

for testimonies.

        Percy was not the only author to feel the sting of

Ritson's jibes.   Pinkerton also was attacked, with vehemence

bordering on brutality, for his collections of songs and ballads,

and particularly for his observations on his material.   Burd

believes that the attack was intensified because of Pinkerton's

nationality, since it is true that to "Scotchmen [Ritson] enter-

tained an aversion as pronounced as that of Dr. Johnson".[45]

But Thomas Warton had been castigated in like manner years

before, for his History of English Poetry (1774-31), the

history in which he gave three chapters to Scottish verse,

thus being the first Englishman to discuss critically and histor-

ically the work of Scottish poets.   No attack, however, was

 more scathing or vindictive than Ritson's uncompromising

denunciation of well-meaning Percy.   Percy, declining to

take public action, tried through private intervention to
make explanations to his critic,/in vain. Ritson would
not be silenced, neither could he be ignored. Ritson was
embarrassingly convincing. Even Percy's admirer, John
Pinkerton, although one who had also suffered at the hands
of Ritson, had finally gone over to the enemy's camp, and
in a letter to Percy admitted the error in his thinking:

I must confess myself thoroughly convinced that Minstrel
only implied Musician, and was never used for a bard, maker
or poet; were I reprinting any former production in this
way I would retract all my opinions to the contrary, though
often repeated.

After suggesting a rearrangement of Percy's essay to distinguish the minstrel proper from the poets and reciters,
Pinkerton added:

Even granting all the passages cited in your favour, you
must contend against hundreds on the opposite side. For a
part, Ritson's book may be referred to.46

        In 1791 a third edition of Ancient and Modern Scot-
ish Songs, Heroic Ballads, etc. appeared, which Thomas
Wilson Bayne, writing in the Dictionary of National Biography, describes as being "manifestly without Herd's
supervision". No fewer than forty-one of Herd's songs were
omitted, and their places supplied by modern compositions,
some of them popular songs by Burns. There was no preface,
and Herd's notes were omitted. While there is no evidence
that Herd offered any objection to this pirating of his text,
or to the misspelling of the word "Scottish", in the title,

it would appear that some readers found the new edition unsatisfactory, and hoped for another. George Chalmers wrote to a friend: "You talked of a new edition of Mr. D. Herd's Songs, to be edited by Mr. W. Scott. Is this almost ready for the public? I hope Mr. Scott will not touch the text."[47] Scott's edition, if it had ever been projected, did not appear -- it will be remembered that he acknowledged the use of Herd's MS. in his own Minstrelsy. More than a hundred years went by before a page for page reprint of the edition of 1776 was published.

In the meantime, three years after the publication in 1791 of Herd's Songs in its mutilated form, a fourth edition of the Reliques was released, but not under the editorship of Bishop Percy. The task of editing, explaining and apologising had been left to a nephew, who was also a name-sake, Thomas Percy.

Do we find once more that Johnson is a dangerous person to disagree with? Was it his criticism that hurt Percy? We remember that it was for the convenience of the great man that Percy had had the folio bound in the first place; and the sad mishap caused by the binder. But we remember also:

Dr. Johnson resisted to the end what he considered a deplorable deviation from neo-classical standards. In 1777, "he observed that a gentleman of eminence in literature had got into a bad style of poetry of late . . . . Boswell: That is owing to his being much versant in Old English Poetry,

Johnson: What is that to the purpose, Sir? If I say a man
is drunk and you tell me it is owing to his taking much
drink, the matter is not mended. No, Sir -- -- has taken
to an odd move." (And he then produced his famous parody:
'Hermit hoar, in solemn cell')". 48

In 1794 Percy's nephew found it still necessary to defend

his relative, and stated in his introduction:

The appeal publicly made to Dr. Johnson in the first page
of the following Preface, so long since as the year 1765,
and never once contradicted by him during so large a portion of his life, ought to have precluded every doubt concerning the existence of the Manuscript in question.

The ~~disinterest~~ indifference may have been due to the venom with which Ritson

had attacked, or it may, though less probably, have been due to

private acknowledgement on the part of Bishop Percy of the

superior quality of Herd's variants of ballads. It may even

have been/grief caused by suffered on the death of his young son, the

son for whom he had destined the folio MS. and of whom he

had great hopes for assistance in this work. Whatever the

cause, the younger editor explained in the "Advertisement"

to the fourth edition:

Twenty years have nearly elapsed since the last edition of
this work appeared. But, although it was sufficiently a
favourite with the public, and had long been out of print,
the original Editor had no desire to revive it .
More important pursuits had, as might be expected, engaged
his attention; and the present edition would have remained
unpublished, had he not yielded to the importunity of his
friends, and accepted the humble offer of an Editor in a
Nephew.

Posterity has not accorded importance to the pursuits in

which the Bishop was engaged in Dromore; his fame rests

solely on the Reliques

The text of 1794 was a great improvement on that of
all previous editions. Percy had not held out against his
critics; and the edition of 1794 is a lesson in how grace-
fully a gentleman who considers it more important to please the
reader than to instruct will accept correction. The famous

him (inserted above "instruct")

essay on minstrels was changed, although all mention of the
changes was relegated to a footnote:

Wedded to no hypothesis, the Author hath readily corrected
any mistakes which have been _proved_ to be in this Essay;
and considering the novelty of the subject, and the time,
and place, when and where he first took it up, many such
had been excusable. -- That the term _minstrel_ was not confined, as some contend, to a mere _musician_, in this country,
any more than on the Continent, will be considered more
fully in the last note . . . at the end of this Essay.

The title of the essay was subtly altered from "An Essay on
the Ancient English Minstrels", to "An Essay on the Ancient
Minstrels in England", and the difficulties of the Anglo-
Saxons and the Normans thus gently overcome. Nor did Percy
any longer insist on the greater antiquity of the minstrels.
The essay began:

The Minstrels were an order of men in the middle ages, who
subsisted by the arts of poetry and music, and sang to the
harp verses composed by themselves, or others. They also
appear to have accompanied their songs with mimickry and
action; and to have practised such various means of divert-
ing as were much admired in those rude times, and supplied
the want of more refined entertainment.

In this way he encompassed the undiscriminating term
"minstrel".

Unfortunately not enough changes were made. The

preface   ury

diction the Bishop was accustomed to use, and the younger
Percy was equally addicted to ambiguity and half-statement:

These volumes are now restored to the public with such
corrections and improvements as have occurred since the
former impression; and the text in particular hath been
emended in many passages by recurring to the old copies.
The instances, being frequently trivial, are not always
noted in the margin, but the alteration hath never been
made without good reason; and especially in such pieces as
were extracted from the folio Manuscript so often mentioned
in the following pages, where any variation occurs from the
former impression, it will be understood to have been given
on the authority of that MS.

Some of Percy's methods of emending the text have
been shown. That he was conscious of the lack of accuracy
is clear from the defence he made of his errors in advanc-
ing lack of proof-reading in extenuation; but as Ritson
had acidly observed, "[Percy] would perceive the justice of
confining this excuse to the first edition".[49] It is
manifestly clear today that Ritson, without access to the
folio MS. was justified in declaring that Percy had "fairly
and honestly printed scarcely one single poem, song or
ballad".[50] Nor was this state of affairs materially mended
by 1794; Percy's position remained in the end what it was
in the beginning -- he believed that the pieces had to be
polished that they might "in the present state of improved
literature be deemed worthy the attention of the public".

The honours on the score of the minstrels are today
as evenly divided as when Scott wrote in the supplement to
the Encyclopedia Britannica:

[U]pon a recent perusal of both these ingenious essays, we
were surprised to find that the reverend editor of the
Reliques and the accurate antiquary have differed so very
little as in essential facts they appear to have done . . . .
[H]ot arguments, and on one side, at least, hard words are
unsparingly employed; while . . . the contest grows warmer
in proportion as the ground concerning which it is carried
on is narrower and more insignificant. In reality their
systems do not essentially differ.[51]

Percy's theory of antiquity was not wholly wrong, nor was

Ritson's theory of the Elizabethan origin of the ballads

wholly right. There is perhaps less unanimity regarding

Ritson's criticism of Bishop Percy's methods of editing the

ballads. Ritson had said:

If the ingenious editor had published all his imperfect
poems by correcting the blunders of puerility or inattention,
and supplying the defects of barbarian ignorance, with
proper distinction of type, it would not only have gratified
the austerest antiquary, but also provided refined entertainment for every reader of taste and genius.[52]

In this Burd agrees with Percy:

Modern critics and historians of literature following
[Percy's] lead, declare with one accord that the plan pursued
was the only one which would have insured a kindly reception
to these rude remains of antiquity.[53]

Nevertheless one can say with Ritson, while apologizing for

his syntax, "As a publication of uncommon elegance and

poetical merit, I have always been, and still am, a warm

admirer of Bishop Percy's Reliques", [54] and continue to agree

with him when he says more strongly:

To correct the errors of an illiterate transcriber, to supply
irremediable defects, and to make sense of nonsense, are
certainly essential duties of an editor of ancient poetry,
provided he act with integrity and publicity; but secretly
to suppress the original text. and insert his own fabrica-
tions fo   nt

for readers of taste and genius, is no proof of either judgment, candor, or integrity.[55]

Proof that the public was not quite so tender-minded with regard to its ballads as Percy and Burd might have us believe is found in the reception accorded to Herd's first volume, which was so rapidly sold out that augmented volumes were published a few years later; and when Herd did not accede to public demand and issue a third edition, the pirated volumes of 1791 went on the market. Herd was, in the particulars given above, an editor after Ritson's own heart. More proof is found in the fact that Ritson's own collections, <u>Ancient Songs</u>, <u>Pieces of Ancient Popular Poetry</u>, <u>English Songs</u> and <u>Scotish Songs</u>, all <u>unbowdlerized</u> and without poetic effort on the part of the editor, were also given a warm welcome. If the charming woodcuts by John and Thomas Bewick which illustrate the first edition <u>of Pieces</u> <u>of Ancient</u> ~~Songs~~ <u>Popular Poetry</u> are adduced as reason for the popularity of Ritson, it may be noted that they are not present in his other volumes. The popularity of the chapbooks by Robert and Andrew Foulis, and nearer the end of the century, of the "penny numbers" published by Brash and Reid, indicate also that the climate of opinion was favourable to "the rude remains of Antiquity" in their unpolished state.

Although Percy may have been wrong in that partic-ular analysis, he remains a man "susceptible to the literary

currents and tendencies of his time". The enthusiam which
had stirred Scotland for the old songs, old poems and old
ballads at the beginning of the century, reasserted itself
more strongly than ever after the publication of Herd's
collections. Indeed the three decades preceding the
publication of Scott's Minstrelsy of the Scottish Border
were extraordinarily rich in the number of volumes test-
ifying to Scottish determination to mine this rediscovered
golden vein. With this delight in vernacular poetry on
the part of the public came a growing demand for historical
and textual accuracy in all matters of antiquarian
interest.

          In 1770 Lord Hailes, Percy's Scottish correspondent,[5]
reproduced in their original state a number of poems from
the Bannatyne manuscript, with the avowed intention of
remedying the inaccuracies of Ramsay's too-free text, an
intention not quite realised,[57] While he included "The
Wife of Auchtermouchtie" in his collection, Hailes stated
that he had omitted popular poems, "The Battle of Harlaw",
"Johnie Armstrang" and "The Ballat of the Reid-Squair",
because they were so well known, a tribute to the popularity of old ballads. In 1777 Thomas Evans published Old
Ballads, Historical and Narrative, with Some of Modern Date;
a mediocre collection, but one in which the compiler shared
the current view that the first printing of a ballad was

Collection of Old Ballads, incorporating the editor's
notes as well. He did not omit "Johny Armstrong's Last
Good-Night", or "Gilderoy" on the score of their too great
familiarity.

The last quarter of the eighteenth century was the
day of the Scottish collector, however, and in 1781 John
Pinkerton published in London, anonymously, but with much
publicity, Scottish Tragic Ballads. Despite Pinkerton's
youthfulness this was not his first excursion into the
field of ballads. In 1776, he wrote two essays, "On the
Oral Tradition of Poetry" and "On the Tragic Ballad", which
together with a dedication, served as the introduction to
Tragic Ballads. He was not content to go back a mere half
century to find poetic tradition: he began with "The
Osiris of the Egyptians, and Apollo of the Greeks"; then
with a passing glance at the Persians, the Jews and the
Druids of Gaul and Britain, he arrived at "the successors
of Ossian", at which point he added a footnote: "For an
account of the more modern minstrels see Dr. Percy's
Dissertation, which is so complete that it leaves nothing
to add". Tragic Ballads was re-issued in 1783 as Select
Scottish Ballads, with the sub-title, Hardy Knute . . . .
with other nine approved Scottish Ballads . . . . . This
not exactly a reprint of the first volume, as some does

were omitted; but the dissertations remained unchanged. Ritson had not yet selected the bludgeon with which he was to smite the reckless author. At this point it is interesting to note that on the copy of Tragic Ballads now in the Bodleian Library, Oxford, Francis Douce wrote on the flyleaf, "Ritson wrote in his copy of this work 'By one Pinkerton. Scotish forgeries and Scotish lies' ". And despite the seeming anonymity of the volume, there is another note in Pinkerton's handwriting, "To Mrs Douce from the Editor".

It should be noted in passing that the compilers of the catalogue 18th-Century Scottish Books are in error in stating that Pinkerton's collection is noteworthy for the first appearance of "Sir James the Rose", as this had already been printed five times. The error is somewhat reprehensible in view of the fact that Pinkerton himself in his notes on the ballad mentioned other printings. As Pinkerton was accurate so seldom, one of the few times he stated a fact should be credited to him. Of a ballad which was his own composition he explained that it was now first published, adding, " whether it has any real foundation, the Editor cannot be positive, though it is very likely." And again, "This affecting piece . . . now appears for the first time". Though technically speaking the truth, Pinkerton was here implying oral tradition for still another of his

own compositions. These notes g ve rise to Ritson's anger,
and Pinkerton ad ed to his offences by st ting in the preface that his b ll ds were "now first publi hed from
tradition in their original perfection". This original
perfection he said he had found in the Maitland collection,
two volumes of manuscript, one a folio d ted from about
1555, the other a quarto dating from 1586. "The Editor"
could not be positive, but as Scott's baronet said in The
Antiquary, "Ritson has no doubts". The folio did exist --
it still does -- and contains among other traditional
songs, two versions of "Lady Anne Bothwell's Lament"
(collated in chapter five); but Ritson was correct in
designating some of the poems "artful and impudent forgeries
in a letter to the Gentleman's Magazine, which he signed
"Anti-Scot". [58]   This letter, however, was shown to Pinkerton
by the editor of the Gentleman's Magazine before it was
published, and the strange situation arose of Pinkerton's
being allowed to print a denial of the charges before they
were made. But Pinkerton was not a very determined liar,
and in his next publication he made full confession. In
"A List of the Scotish Poets", prefixed to his Ancient
Scotish Poems, 1786, he was both modest and disarming,
although modesty is a quality which sits oddly on this
precocious scholar. The specious quality of the composition
almost excuses Ritson's anger. In it Pinkerton requested
pardon b   he

fiction with regard to Hardyknute] to himself:

The fiction, as the publisher can inform, could not possibly
have any sordid view, as the MS. was presented to him, and
one half the future profits, which was offered, was refused.
For the imposition, it was only meant to give pleasure to
the public; and no vanity could be served where the name
was unknown . . . . Perhaps, like a very young man as he
was, he had pushed one or two points of the deception a
little too far; but he always thought th t novel and poetry
has NO BOUNDS of fiction.

He had said that he could not be positive as to the real

foundations of "The Laird of Woodhouslie", but now since he

is in the confessional he must admit that he wrote it him-

self, and of some others he said that they were "one half

from tradition, one half by the editor; tho he could not

now distinguish the lines".

Ritson was not easily mollified, nd obviously dis-

trusted the repentance. In his "Historical Essay on

Scotish Song", 1794, he lashed out again:

Had this letter (upon which the editor [of the Gentleman's
Magazine] out of his singular urbanity, allowed the culprit
the extraordinary privilege of making false and evasive his
comments previous to its publication) never ap eared, these
contemptible forgeries would have continued to disgrace the
annals of Scotish poetry till, at least, the pretence of
antiquity had proved too slight a buoy to support the
weight of their intrinsic dulness. [20]

Notwithstanding the singularity of his syntax and spelling,

Ritson had made himself clear.

Ancient Scotish Poems, which does not contain any

ballads, was prefaced by a formidable body of prose. This

is a work more remarkable as a literary curiosity than as

critical or historical material. It is worthy of note only

in that it gave Ritson added impetus to compile collections
of Scottish songs and ballads for the purpose of showing how
wrong Pinkerton could be. Ritson could not only tell that
the furrow was crooked, he could show how to plough one
straight. Pinkerton, on the other hand, saw the crookedness
but was incapable of showing how the work should be done.
In the preface to his Ancient Scotish Poems he castigated
Evans' Old Ballads in a diatribe worthy of Ritson, stating
that Evans' book was "fraught with the merest trash that
ever disgraced the press". Less easily excused is his un-
critical statement that the careful painstaking Herd was "an
illiterate and injudicious compiler".[60]

Still another collection which came from the Scottish presses in the eighties is G. Caw's Poetical Museum,
which anticipated Johnson's title by a few years. Caw's
collection was not remarkable. The editor, who was also
the printer, stated on the title page that it contained
"Songs and Poems on almost every Subject". It is full of
eighteenth-century pastorals, poems by Thomson and Shenstone,
and ditties and odes by anonymous authors. The title page
is dated MDCCLXXXIV, and the preface signed "G.C." is dated
"Hawick, Sept. 15, 1784", but underneath an engraving
opposite the title page, the legend reads "Edin...1792".
Such ballads as the volume contains were taken from Pinkerton's Scotish Tragic Ballads and the notes are almost word

for word reprints of the same text. Of interest is Caw's spelling, which has at times reverted to that of the old makars.

A more significant collection, generally assigned to James Johnson, was The Scots Musical Museum, a repository of many of Burns's finest lyrics and adaptations of ballads. This began to appear in 1787, and continued for several years until six volumes in all had been published. These contained both words and music, as had Orpheus Caledonius sixty years earlier; and in 1794 this procedure was also followed by Ritson. In 1790 a firm of printers and book-sellers, R. Morison and Son, of Perth, brought out A Select Collection of favourite Scotish Ballads in four volumes. This was another reprint of Pinkerton's text, but the Morisons did not feel it necessary to become more archaic in spelling than did Pinkerton himself, whom they treated with reverent admiration, and to whom they made humble acknowledgement of their indebtedness. No new ballads appeared in these volumes, and they contain many poems which are not ballads. Almost at the end of the century two publishers, Brash and Reid, brought out at frequent inter-vals little booklets of poems similar to the chapbooks of Robert and Andrew Foulis. They consisted of eight pages and were sold for one penny each. Since they met with a ready sale, twenty-four of them were brought together and

published in book form with a general title page and a
table of contents. A year later thirty-one more "penny
numbers" were brought together and published. Brash and
Reid published in all ninety-nine booklets of poems, among
which were a considerable number of ballads. Their work,
while not up to the standard set by the Foulis brothers,
shows textual accuracy and the use of fairly good paper and
clear type.[61]

In 1794 Ritson published Scotish Song, the pleasant
song-book of words and music already referred to. Prefixed
to this volume is the interesting "Dissertation on the
Scottish Music" by William Tytler, quoted by song collectors
for half a century. Ritson could occasionally accord praise
and he said of Tytler's notes, "The following observations,
by a late ingenious writer, already quoted, have been
thought too pertinent and valuable to be either omitted or
abridged".[62] In a footnote referring to Tytler's dissertation Ritson explained his spelling of "Scottish". Since
Ritson's spelling was widely copied, the explanation is
given here:

The word Scottish is an improper orthography of Scotish;
Scotch is still more corrupt, and Scots (as an adjective)
a national barbarism: which is observed here once for all,
to prevent the imputation of inconsistency and confusion;
as a direct quotation should be always literal.[63]

Walter Scott said of Ritson that he "brought forward such a work on national antiquities as in other
countries has been thought worthy of universities and the
countenanc

seek, but universities have indeed given him attention.
Scott himself may have listened to Ritson, but he went his
own way in the matter of ballad transcribing; and it was
not until Motherwell in 1827 put forth his views, that
modern standards became the acknowledged practice.

In these remarks on ballad collecting and ballad
collectors in the eighteenth century, I have tried to show
the changes and advances made both in criticism and collecting by the major figures in this field. The actual changes
which took place in a single ballad from one printing to
the next will be shown in the following chapters when two
ballads will be collated. For the purpose of this thesis
it was necessary to chose two on which not much work had
been done. Child, of course, compiled a great body of information on the ballads in his collection, and our debt to
him is immeasurable; but since he made selective and
qualitative judgments on the ballads he used, few in his
collection can be said to have been collated in the way now
attempted. An attempt is made here to show what happened
from one printing to the next.

The first ballad I have chosen to collate is "Captain
Car, or, Edom O' Gordon". My reasons are first, that it is
one of the few ballads Ritson acknowledged to have been of
minstrel origin. Second, it is one of the best of the semi-
historical ballads; and not from the border country, but

from Aberdeenshire, the part of Scotland which, legends of
the border notwithstanding, produced the great part of the
Scottish ballads, including many of the best of them. The
third reason I have chosen this ballad is that in Ian A.
Gordon's Shenstone's Miscellany are to be found, never before printed, Shenstone's versions of both "Edom of Gordon"
and "Captain Carre". The fourth reason is that the ballad
affords a delightful example of Percy's retouching, his
afterthought and careful withdrawal and his final decision.

The second I have chosen for examination is "Lady
Anne Bothwell's Lament", or "Balow". This is the only
ballad in Watson's Collection; therefore it is the earliest
printed ballad which is not a broadsheet or stall copy.
Also it is not in Child's The English and Scottish Popular Ballads
1882-1898, although it is in English and Scottish Ballads
1857-1859. Both the subject matter of this ballad and its
history have been much discussed, and each ballad editor
in turn has given his version of both text and history, with
the exception of Herd, who did not write about his ballads.
It is not known why Child left it out of his large collection. According to ballad criteria it has more right to be
there than several ballads he did include. If it is a
lullaby, it is also a lament, as is "The Bonny Earl of
Murray", and "Bonny George Campbell". If it lacks a strong

Allan"; all of which proves only that there is no infallible method of deciding what is a ballad.

The ballad has been given in full only when t n ve been important changes, such as substitution of stanzas, changes in position of stanzas, omissions or additions to the text. Such changes as variations in spelling or punctuation n ve merely b en mentioned.

Inclusion of the diverse notions of the history of each ballad has perhaps made my text unduly long, but when it is remembered that whole volumes, such as "Edward" and "Sven i Rosengard" by Archer Taylor and Sir Aldingar by P. Christopherson, have been dedicated to studies of single ballads, it will be realised that much con nsation has been achieved in order to compress the studies of "Edom o Gordon" and "Lady Anne Bothwell's Lament" into two chapters.

PART II

Chapter four

"CAPTAIN CAR, OR, EDOM O GORDON"

"The duty of a collator", said Dr. Johnson, "is
indeed dull, yet, like other tedious tasks, is very
necessary."[1]   It should be added that he also remarked,
"The collator's province is safe nd easy, the conjecturer's
perilous and difficult."[2]   But even in the process of
collating, as Dr. Johnson himself must have discovered,
curious results often emerge.

"Edom o Gordon" is a ballad which well illustrates
the editorial methods of the great ballad collectors of
the eighteenth century. It is also notable for being one
of the first dated ballads to describe in song an incident
in Scottish history -- an incident which was also recorded
in prose by contemporary writers. A manuscript of a ballad
telling the story of the burning of Towie House, the seat
of the Forbes in Aberdeenshire, in 1571, is identified in
the British Museum as belonging to the last quarter of the
sixteenth century. Therefore the ballad may well have
been composed by a minstrel within whose memory the incident
occurred. Since the history of the event is well known, and
is discussed in detail by Professor Child in The English and
Scottish Popular Ballads, it is unnecessary to retell it

here. Examination of the history will be confined to the
notes prefixed by ballad editors to the variants investigated.

The method adopted for this discussion is the
presentation of each text in chronological order of
appearance, or, in the case of manuscript, of discovery.
The first text, published in 1755, was a small quarto of
twelve pages printed by Robert and Andrew Foulis of Glasgow. The version had been supplied orally, under the supervision of Sir David Dalrymple. Although the printers
endeavoured to preserve archaisms in diction and in spelling, there is in fact no consistency in either. The metre
has not been eased into smoothness, nor is there always
correspondence of rhyme with rhyme: two qualities generally
present when attempt at improvement of a traditional version
is made. Following their usual custom, the Foulis brothers
did not add notes or explanations to the ballad, nor make
conjectures concerning its origin. It will be noticed that
the text which Child reproduces from the Foulis brothers'
chapbook does not accord in all particulars with that which
now follows. The latter was taken from the original chapbook, now in the University of Toronto Library. The differences are insignificant, a matter of italics, and minor
changes in spelling and punctuation:

EDOM OF GORDON; an ancient Scottish Poem.
Never before printed. R. & A. Foulis, 1755.

It fell about the Martinmas:
Cuhen the wind blew schrile and cauld,
Said Edom o' Gordon to his men,
We maun draw to a hald:

And what an a hald sall we draw to,
My merry men and me?
We will gae to the house of the Rhodes,
To see that fair lady.

She had nae sooner busked her sell,
Nor putten on hir gorn,
Till Edom o Gordon and his men
Were round about the town.

They had nae sooner sitten dovn,
Nor sooner said the grace,
Till Edom o Gordon and his men
Were closed about the place.

The lady ran up to her tower-head,
As fast as she could drie,
To see if by her fair speeches
She could with him agree,

As soon he saw the lady fair
And hir yates all locked fast,
He fell into a rage of wrath,
And his heart was aghast.

Cum down to me, ze lady fair,
Cum down to me; let's see;
This night ze's ly by my ain side,
The morn my bride sall be.

I winnae cum down, ze fals Gordon,
I winnae cum down to thee;
I winnae forsake my ane dear lord,
That is sae far frae me.

Gi up zour house, ze lady fair,
Gi up zour house to me,
Or I will burn zoursel therein,
Bot and zour babies three.

81

I winnae gie up, zou fals Gordon,
To nae sik traitor as thee;
Tho you should burn mysel therein,
Bot and my babies three.

Set fire to the house, quoth fals Gordon,
Sin better may nae bee,
And I will burn hersel therein,
Bot and her babies three.

And ein, wae worth ze, Jock my man,
I paid ze weil zour fee;
Quhy pow ze out the ground wa stane,
Lets in the reek to me?

And ein wae worth ze Jock my man,
I paid ze weil zour hire:
Quhy pow ze out the ground wa stane
To me lets in the fire?

Ze paid me weil my hire, lady,
Ze paid me weil my fee:
But now I'm Edom of Gordon's man,
Maun either do or die.

O then bespake her youngest son,
Sat on the nurses knee,
Dear mother, gie owre your house, he says,
For the reek it worries me.

I winnae gie up my house, my dear,
To nae sik traitor as he;
Cum well, cum wae, my jewels fair,
Ye maun tak share wi me.

O then bespake her dochter dear,
She was baith jimp and sma:
O row me in a pair o' sheits,
And tow me owre the wa.

They rowd her in a pair o' sheits,
And towd her owre the wa:
But on the point of Edom's speir,
She gat a deadly fa.

O bonny, bonny was hir mouth,
And chirry were her cheiks,
And clear, clear was hir zellow hair,
Whereon the reid bluid dreips.

82

Then wi' his speir he turn'd hir owr,
O gin hir face was wan!
He said zou are the first that eer
I wist alive again.

He turn'd hir owr and owr again,
O gin hir skin was whyte!
I might ha spard thy life
To been some mans delyte.

Busk and boon, my merry men all,
For ill dooms I do guess:
I cannae luik in that bonny face,
As it lyes on the grass.

Them luiks to freits, my master deir,
Then freits vill follow them:
Let it neir be said brave Edom o' Gordon
Was daunted with a dame.

O then he spied hir ain deir lord,
As he came owr the lee;
He saw his castle in a fire,
As far as he could see.

Put on, put on, my mighty men,
As fast as ye can drie;
For he that is hindmost of my men,
Sall neir get guid o me.

And some they raid, and some they ran,
Fu fast out owr the plain;
But lang, lang, eer he could get up,
They were a' deid and slain.

But mony were the Mudie men
Lay gasping on the grien;
For o' fifty men that Edom brought out
There were but five ged heme.

And mony were the Mudie men
Lay gasping on the grien,
And mony were the fair ladys
Lay lemanless at heme.

And round, and round the waes he vent;
Their ashes for to view;
At last into the flames he flev,
And bad the world adieu.

us our next piece of information about this ball d. The
publication in 1952 of Shenstone's Miscellany 1759-1763
by Ian A. Gordon adds much-needed information, and makes
more apparent than ever the desirability of bringing into
print all of Percy's voluminous letters and papers. Professor Gordon makes public for the first time Shenstone's
versions of "Edom o Gordon" and "Captain Car", the latter
the English version of the Scottish ballad, both of which
are most illuminating as showing Percy and Shenstone at
work. They reveal even more clearly how large a part Shenstone played in ballad collecting and improving, and, it
appears in this particular case, show up Percy's somewhat
niggardly acknowledgment of the extent of Shenstone's work.

A letter from Shenstone received by Percy in
December 1758 mentions for the first time the Percy folio:
"Mr. Pitt of Shifnal . . . says he gave you those old
ballads."[3] A few months later Percy wrote to Shenstone asking to see the "Improvements of Edom of Gordon",[4] to which
Shenstone replied: "Edom of Gordon, of which you desire a
copy, must receive great alteration towards the Close, before I can endure that you should see it."[5] Professor
Gordon refers to this exchange of letters when he states
in his notes in the Miscellany: "Edom of Gordon was sent
by Percy to Shenstone in 1759 (cf. B.M. Add. 28221, 9 August

1759). Shenstone began on his leisurely task of 'retouching' " [6] Confusion arises here regarding the title of the
ballad. It is remembered that no manuscript exists with
the title "Edom of Gordon" -- this was the title given by
the Glasgow printers. Percy's folio MS., from which he
took the ballad, gives the poem minus a title; but Percy
refers to it as "Captain Carre", from the name of the pro-
tagonist. It is known that Percy occasionally tore out a
handful of sheets from his folio MS. and sent them to a
friend for deciphering or improving. Now we may ask, had
he already followed this procedure with "Captain Carre" and
sent it to Shenstone, calling it "Edom of Gordon", as he
was later to do when he published his version of the ballad
in the Reliques? If he had not done this in 1759, how then
can Professor Gordon's notes be explained?

In 1761 he [Shenstone] is writing to John McGowan, a
'Writer', or solicitor, in Edinburgh, asking for 'any old
Scotch Ballads' (Letters I, 595-9). McGowan . . . apparently sent him the first published edition of Edom of Gordon,
printed by Foulis of Glasgow in 1755. From this Shenstone
with assistance from the Folio Manuscript proceeded to con-
struct his text. He wrote to McGowan enthusiastically:
'He [Percy] shewed me an old ballad in his folio MS., under
the name of Adam Carre: three parts in four coincide so
much with your Edom of Gordon that the former name seems to
me an odd corruption of the latter. His MS. will tend to
enrich Edom of Gordon with two of the prettiest stanzas I
ever saw' (Letters I, 598).[7]

But this was in 1761. As has been noted, three years
earlier Shenstone had discussed the ballad with Percy, and
had not Percy already suggested the "odd corruption" of the

name in calling his b ll d "Edom of Gor on"? It m y be
that hen Shenstone spoke to McGo. n of "your Edom of
Gordon", he w s merely referring to the Scottish version
and this use of "your" would be reason ble when addressed
to a Scotsman. That he did mingle "A m Carre" and " dom
of Gordon" we know -- rofessor Gor on calls the result
"Shenstone's invention", hen he an lyses the result to
show the source of each st nza. The manuscri t which
Shenstone sa , as transcribed by Hales nd Furniv ll in
<u>Bisho Percy's Folio Manuscri t</u>, follows:

> "ffaith, Master, whither you will,
>   whereas you like the best,
> vnto the castle of Bittons borrow,
>   and there to take your rest."
>
> "rut yonder stands a C stle faire,
>   is made of lyme & stone,
> yonder is in it a fayre lady,
>   her lord is ridden & gone."
>
> The lady stood on her castle wall,
>   she looked vpp and downe,
> she was ware of an hoast of men
>   c me rydinge towards the towne.
>
> "See you not, my merry men all,
>   & see you not what I doe see?
> Methinks I see a hoast of Men;
>   I muse who they shold be."
>
> She thought it had beene her louly Lord,
>   he had come ryding home:
> it was the traitor, C t ine Carre,
>   the Lord of westerton towne.

They had noe sooner super sett,
  & after said the grace,
but the traitor Captaine Carre
  was light about the place.

"Giue over thy house, thou Lady gay,
  I will make thee a band,
all night with-in mine armes thoust Lye,
  to-morrow be the heyre of my Land."

"Ile not giue over my house," shee said,
  "neither for Ladds nor man,
nor yet for traitor Captaine Carre,
  vntill my lord Come home;

But reach me my pistoll pee,
  & charge you well my gunne,
Ile shoote at the bloody bucher,
  the lord of westerton."

She stood vppon her castle wall
  & let the bulletts flee,
and where shee mist . . . .

        (half a page missing.)

But then bespake the litle child
  that sate on the nurses knee,
saies, "mother deere, giue ore this house,
  for the smoake it smoothers me."

"I wold giue all my gold, my childe,
  soe wold I doe all my fee,
for one blast of the westerne wind
  to blow the smoke from thee."

But when shee saw the fier
  came flaming ore her head,
shee tooke then vpp her children 2,
  Sayes, "babes, we all beene dead!"

But Adam then he fired the house,
  a sorrowfull sight to see:
now hath he burned this lady faire
  & eke her children 3.

Then Captaine Carre he rode away,
  he staid noe longer at that tide,
he thought that place it was to warme
  soe neere for to abide;

87

He called vnto his merry men all,
  bidd them make hast away,
"for we haue slaine his children 3,
  all, & his Lady gay."

Home came to louly London on,
  to London wheres her lord lay,
This castle & his hall was burned
  all, & his lady gay.

Soe hath he done his Children 3,
  more dearer vnto him
than either the siluer or the gold
  that men soe faine wold win."

But when he looket this writing on,
  Lord, in is hart he was woe!
saies, "I will find thee, Captaine Carre,
  wether thou ryde or goe!

"Buske yee, borne yee, my merrymen all,
  with tempered swords of steele,
for till I haue found out Captaine Carre,
  my hart it is nothing weele."

But when he came to dractons borro.,
  soe long ere it was day,
& ther he found him, Captaine Carre;
  that night he went to stay.

        (half a page missing.)

    Shenstone copied the foregoing into his Miscellany
with only the slightest changes. He called it "Captain
Carre", and underneath added "A Fragment from Mr. Percy's
Collection of Old Ballads". In his notes he stated: "This
ballad and Edom of Gordon seem founded on the same story;
and it is possible to frame an admirable poem out of
both."[8] Since the changes he made are unimportant, being
only alterations in spelling and punctuation, his text is not

transcribed here.

　　The "admirable poem" framed out of both, however,
was in a different case. Shenstone kept the title "Edom
of Gordon", and beneath it wrote "From the Edition printed
at Glasgow, corrected and enlarg'd by help of Mr. Percy's
old english M.S. [sic] Professor Gordon points out that the
Miscellany contains notes in Shenstone's handwriting; and
as the manuscript remained in Percy's hands for many years
after Shenstone's death in 1763, there are in addition
notes in Percy's handwriting. The poem is given here as
Shenstone left it:

Edom of Gordon

It fell out about Martin-mas,
　　Quhen the wind blew schrile & cauld,
Said Edom o' Gordon to his men,
　　We maun draw to a hauld.

And to what kind of hauld sall we,
　　My merry men, repair?
We will gae to the house of the Rhodes
　　To see that Lady fair.

Lo yonder appears the castle tall
　　Those tours of antient Fame
And in them dwells a peerless dame
　　Her Lord far gone frae hame.

The Ladye she stood on her Castle wall
　　Beheld baith dale & down
And there she was ware of an host of men
　　Came troopinge towards the town.

O! see you not, my merry men all,
  O see not you, what I see?
Methinketh I see an Houst of men
  I muse, who they should be.

She deem'd it had been her lovely Lord
  All merrily prauncing hame
But it was the traitor Edom o' Gordon
  That recat nae sin, nor shame.

She had nae sooner busket her sell
  Nor putten on her gown
Till Edom o' Gordon & his men
  Were round about the town.

They had nae sooner the supper sett
  Nae sooner said the grace
Till Edom o' Gordon & his men
  Were closed about the Place.

The Ladye ran up to her tower head
  As fast as she coud flee
To try if by her speeches fair
  She could with him agree

As soon as he saw this Lady bright
  And hir yates all locked fast
He fell into a rage of wrath
  And his Look was all aghast.

Give owr thy house thou Lady gay
  And thou sallt mine command
Give owr thy house, & eer sun-rise
  Thoust be the Heyre o' my Land.

Come down to me, ye Lady fair,
  And let me thy Levtie see
This night ye's ly by my ain side
  Tomorrow, my bride sall be.

I winnae gi owr my house, she said,
  Whoe'er sall make the claim;
Much less for traitorous Edom o' Gordon
  Before my Lord come hame

I winnae come down, ye fals Gordon
  I winnae come down to thee
I winnae forsake my ain dear Lord
  That is sae far frae me.

Gi up your house, ye Lady fair;
  Gi up your house to me;
Or I will burn yoursel therein,
  Bot and your babies three

I winnae gie up thou fals Gordon
  To nae sik traitor as thee
Tho you should turn mysel therein
  Bot and my babies three

But reach me my Pistol, Glaud, my man,
  Or deftly charge my gun
For unless I pierce this Bucher's hart
  My husband is undone.

She stood upon her castle wall,
  And let the bullets flee;
But ah, they mist the traitor's hart,
  And only raz'd his knee.

Set fire to the house, quoth fals Gordon,
  Sin better may nae bee;
And I will burn hersel therein
  Bot and her babies three

And ein, wae worth ye Jock my man,
  I paid ye well your fee,
Why pow ye out my ground-wa stane
  Lets in the reek to me

And ein, wae worth ye Jock my man
  I paid you well your hire,
Why pow ye out my ground-wa stane
  To me lets in the Fire.

Ye paid me well my Fee & Hire,
  Sweet Ladie, I not deny;
But now I'm Edom o' Gordon's man
  Maun either do, or die.

O then bespake her youngest child,
  That sate on nurse's knee
My mother dear gie owre this house
  For the reek it worries me.

I wold gie all my gold, my childe
  So wold I, all my Fee
For one blast of the westerne winde
  To blow this reek from thee

91

But I mauna gie up my house, my dear
   To nae sik traitor as He
Cum weall, cum wae, my Jewells fair
   Ye maun take share wi me.

O then bespake her Dochter dear
   She was baith jimp & sma
O row me in a pair of sheets
   And tow me owre the wa

They row'd her in a pair of sheets
   And tow'd her owre the wa
But on the point of Edom's spear
   She gat a deadly Fa.

O bonny bonny was her mouth
   An chirry were her cheiks
And clear clear was hir yellow hair
   Whereon the reid bluid dreips.

Then wi his speir he turn'd her owr
   O gin hir face was wan
He said, you are the first that eer
   I wist alive again.

He turn'd her owr & ow'r again
   O gin her skin was white,
He said, I might ha spard thy Life
   To been some man's delight.

Busk & boon, my merry men all,
   For ill dooms I do guess --
I cannae behold that bonny Face
   That does the græn-sward press.

Them Luiks to freits, my master dear
   Then Freits will follow them
Let it neir be said brave Edom o' Gordon
   Was daunted by a Dame --

Now when this Ladye saw the Fire
   Come flaming oer her head
She lifted up her children twain --
   Ah me! my babes beene dead!

Thus Edom o' Gordon fir'd the House
   A sorrowfull sight to see
Now hath he burned this Lady fair
   Bot and her babies three

92

Now worde was brought to London-to n,
  Whereas her husband lay,
That Edom o' Gordon had burnt his hall
  Bot and his Lady gay

Soe hath he done his children three
  Each one more deare to Him
Than silver, gold, and Jewells vere,
  Or his most precious Limb.

But when he luikt the Letter owre
  Good Lord! his hart was woe
Yes Edom o' Gordon, thy Life is mine
  Where'er thou ryde or goe.

Butte ye, bowne ye, my merry men all
  With tempered swords of steele
For 'till I have met with Edom o' Gordon
  My hart is nothing weele.

But when he came to Bitton's borrow,
  Sae lang e'er it was day;
They pray'd their Lord to litt & eat --
  But he maun gang away.

Now traiterous Edom was hors'd & gone
  Nae loitering at this tide
Nae place of safety there for him
  Or for his train to bide

He called up his merry men all
  And bade them haste away
For we have slain his children three
  Bot & his Lady gay

O then he spied her ain dear Lord,
  As he came owr the Lee,
Who saw his castle in a blaze;
  As far as he mought see.

Put on put on my mighty men
  As fast as ye can drie
For he, that's hindmost of my train
  Sall neir get guid of me.

And some they raid, & some they ran
  Fu' fast out owr the plain
But lang lang e'er they sped frae hame
  Baith Lady & babes were slain

Yet mony were the Mudie men
Appeas'd thilk infant's claim;
For o' fifty men that Edom brought
There were but five ged hame

A sacrifice of equal Price
Was offered to the Dame
And many were the Ladies fair
Lay Lemanless at hame.

Then round & round the waes he went
Their ashes for to view
At last he rushd into the Flames
And bade the world adieu.

The Foulis text has 29 stanzas, the Percy MS. has

21, and Shenstone's version has 47. Professor Gordon has
    (with one slight inaccuracy, shown in note 9, p. 167)
worked out/the following table showing Shenstone's fusion

of the two ballads, and his own additions. The numbers

refer to the stanzas in the Miscellany text. (Captain

Carre, C.; Foulis edition, F.; Shenstone's invention, W.S.):

1-2	.	.	F.	13	.	. C.	33-39	. . C.
3	.	.	.W.S.	14-16	.	. F.	40-41	. .W.S.
4-6	.	.	. C.	17-18	.	C.;W.S.	42-45	. . F.
				19-23	.	. F.		
7-10	.	.	. F.	24	.	.W.S.	46	. . E;W.S.
11	.	.	. C.	25-32	.	. F.	47	. . . F.
12	.	. E;W.S. 9						

The next piece of information we have concerning the ballad

is found in a letter from Percy to Dalrymple, written on

December 2, 1762. "I have obtained copies of several very

poetical old ballads published within these few years at

Glasgow viz. . . . Edom of Gordon."[10] Dalrymple's reply to

this letter has not been found, but on January 7, 1763,

Percy wrote:

I am extremely happy to find I have the pleasure of
corresponding with the Editor of Edom of Gordon, it gives
me an opportunity of proposing some queries on that Subject. In my ancient MS Collection of Old ballads (a large
folio Vol. containing near 600 pages very closely writt.)
is a fragment of a very pathetic old Ballad, that evidently is upon the same subject, altho' the Idiom is English
and the names of persons and places different: The tyrant
of this piece is named Adam Carre which is not very remote
from Edom o' Gordon. -- I have inclosed a Copy for your
Inspection. I think if a few of the Stanzas were to be
reduced to Scottish Idiom and inserted in your Scottish
Ballad, they would contribute to its improvement, particularly that fine stroke of the Pathos.

> "I wolde give all my golde, my child,
> "Soe wolde I doe all my fee.
> "For one blast of the westerne wind
> "To blow the smoke from thee.

. . . Be pleased, Sir, to inform me whence you had Edom
of Gordon.

That Dalrymple must have replied is obvious from the letter

which follows, but the reply is missing. On January 25,

1763, Percy wrote:

Permit me . . . to thank you for your curious Strictures
on Adam Carre and Edom of Gordon, and the amusing Landscape
you have drawn of the Country of Ballad-singing: all hints
of this kind will be of use to me and will enrich my preface
But permit me to beg that you will not let the subject rest
here: The Editor of Edom of Gordon I hope will new digest
that ballad by inserting whatever he thinks valuable in the
other.[11]

How much Percy used of the "amusing Landscape" will be

seen in the preface to the ballad, as he printed it in 1765.

Shenstone had died in the meantime and Percy had continued

to work on the ballad. On February 11, 1764, he wrote to

Dalrymple:

It is now a long time that I have been indebted to you for a most obliging letter. The constant demands of the press (which is now hastening our work to a conclusion must be my excuse. Inclosed I send a proof for your inspection; and, what is of more consequence, a new Edition of your own Ballad of Edom o' Gordon, for your approbation I know not how far you will admit the alterations and enlargements: they were in some measure pointed out by my late friend Mr. Shenstone, who left among his papers some hints how and where he could wish the alterations might be made. If I have not sufficiently succeeded in Scotifying the English stanzas, I beg your unsparing corrections. -- The 22d and 23d stanzas, I do not understand, and think if they were wholly thrown out, the poem would hasten more rapidly to a conclusion. What is the meaning of Luiks to freits, &c? Perhaps I only condemn, like all other criticks, because I do not understand.

I have also sent a rude first-draught of the Preface I propose to prefix to this ballad: You will see to whom I am indebted, for the curious particulars of which it is composed: I think you forbade me pointing out too particularly, what exact matters of information I received from you, I have therefore reserved the acknowledgment of these kind favours for my general Preface to the Work. Be pleased to correct the inclosed introduction, and alter it ad libitum . . . .
PS   May I intreat that Edom o' Gordon may speedily return? -- Mr. Dodsley desires the 2 first Volumes may be seen by no eyes but your own. -- I am afraid the last line of stanz. 31. of Edom o' Gordon, is not true Scots Idiom. Should it not be "He wreiked his teen, for the loss of his lady:" or &c.[12]

Within three weeks Percy was eagerly acknowledging Dal-

rymple's prompt assistance, if not quite agreeing with all

the suggestions made for improvement:

I lose not a moment in acknowledging the favour of your last; I will not fail to insert the two stanzas them luiks to freits &c, now you have taught me to understand them; pray should not the two lines stand thus?

Thame luiks to freits, my master dear,
x The freits will follow thame:
          or
x Then freits will follow thame:

i.e. them, that look after omens, the omens will follow TH

th; as the judicious interpreter ole to ex p's the rief
.gamemnon roperly, covered it fro his . he sle
l end very ell, t

   nd ony were t e wei l   een
   hey lemonless t emo.

.dislike my two stanzas; but I think so   su   li
s

  in word wi' f l certain

ld be inserted, if we retain   h sh ne's   t t ?
ing, but s ppos ing t at is rief and re i is-
oted, o account or much   irc um nt;   u ft   ll,
ks like a modern, a tificiel cotri do: n   ill
ays lo k so, ex re s it how we will.

I am content to ive u __in_ -- provided you ll
ase to favour me wit   betterthon tc n o: t n ri n.--
old oets were s tisf -d rovid d t   sowel c r ed-
ded; ven if the ndi ents we e di e t: u ld
it ed a total   lesimllitude of oth . . . .

s I shall never ention   w   it rd to

t ste field's _ on ut; w ic indo d I sw d
r ands; I wish you ould permit to n t l it. --
r sentiment of   e   ndon on t at s ne oets   ,
 rll c ntinue un less, unk w   to st   er:
I promise u on my onour it a li b.   e u , t t
ever gave me t   lest int o t at subject . . . .

> You will find t e word nes   lied t   arriers in

Dalrymple's letter is missing, but the conclusion Percy so much disliked has been saved. In Ap endix III of the <u>Percy-Dalrymple Correspondence</u>, Falconer reproduces it as follows:

Hailes's Contributions to the <u>Reliques</u>: Canceled Before Publication

In Percy's own copy of the <u>Reliques</u> (now in the Harvard University Library) occur four additional stanzas of "Edom o' Gordon" contributed by Lord Hailes. In this copy, p. 107 (H_6^r) of Vol. III (Vol. I in Percy's subsequent rearrangement) contains the following stanzas:

> And mony wer the mudie men,
>   Lay gasping on the grèin:
> For o' fifty men, that Edom brocht out,
>   But five returnd again.
>
> And mony were the mudie men,
>   He left to grin and grane:
> And mony were the weiping dames,
>   Lay lemanless at hame.
>
> Then back to his lady and babes he hied,
>   Their esches dear to find:
> Ah! lever I'd find those dear eschès,
>   Than a' the gowd of Inde.
>
> And round, and round the wa's he went
>   Ein wood wi' fell despair:
> Then lap into the brenning flames,
>   And word spaik nevir mair.

Across the top of the page, Percy has written: "The follow^g Sta^s by Sr David Dalrymple were rejected."[16]

Professor Gordon has stated that Percy's earliest proof sheets show that for his first printed version he used the Foulis text,[17] and Professor Gordon does not mention the above stanzas. But the search for the ashes has no counterpart in the Foulis version; and the final stanza

in the latter is starkly simple; contrasting favourably
with the sentimentality in Hailes's version.

"Edom o' Gordon", as Percy finally decided to print
it in the Reliques of 1765, is now given along with the
preface incorporating Dalrymple's hints as to landscape:

Edom o' Gordon

--was printed at Glasgow, by Robert and Andrew Foulis,
MDCCLV, 8 vo. 12 pages. -- We are indebted for its publication (with many other valuable things in these volumes) to
Sir David Dalrymple, Bart. who gave it as it was preserved
in the memory of a lady, that is now dead.
        The reader will here find it improved, and enlarged
with several fine stanzas, recovered from a fragment of the
same ballad, in the Editor's folio MS. It is remarkable
that the latter is intituled CAPTAIN ADAM CARRE, and is in
the English idiom. But whether the author was English or
Scotch, the difference originally was not great. The English
Ballads are generally of the North of England, the Scottish
are of the South of Scotland, and of consequence the country
of Ballad-singers was sometimes subject to one crown, and
sometimes to the other, and most frequently to neither.
Most of the finest old Scotch songs have the scene laid
within 20 miles of England; which is indeed all poetic
ground, green hills, remains of woods, clear brooks. The
pastoral scenes remain: Of the rude chivalry of former
ages happily nothing remains but the ruins of the castles,
where the more daring and successful robbers resided. The
Castle of the Rhodes is fixed by tradition in the neighbour-
hood of Dunse in Berwickshire. The Gordons were anciently
seated in the same county. Whether this ballad hath any
foundation in fact, we have not been able to discover. It
contains however but too just a picture of the violences
practised in the feudal times all over Europe.
        From the different titles of this ballad, it should
seem that the old strolling bards or minstrels (who gained
a livelihood by reciting these poems) made no scruple of
changing the names of the personages they introduced, to
humour their hearers. For instance, if a Gordon's conduct
was blameworthy in the opinion of that age, the obsequious
minstrel would, when among Gordons, change the name to Car,
whose clan or sept lay further west, and vice versâ . . . .
        It may be proper to mention, that in the English
copy, instead of the "Castle of the Rhodes," it is the

99

"Castle of Bittons-borrow" (or "Diactours-borrow," for it
is very obscurely written) and "Capt. Adam Carre" is called
the "Lord of Westerton-town." Uniformity required that the
additional stanzas supplied from that copy should be cloth-
ed in the Scottish orthography and idiom: this has therefore been attempted, though perhaps imperfectly.

It fell about the Martinmas,
Quhen the wind blew schrile and cauld,
Said Edom o' Gordon to his men,
We maun draw to a hauld:

And quhat a hauld sall we draw to
My mirry men and me?
We wul gae to the house o' the Rhodes,
To see that fair ladie.

The lady stude on hir castle wa',
Beheld baith dale and dovn;
There sne was ware of a host of men
Cum ryding towards the toun.

O see ze nat my mirry men a?
O see ze nat quhat I see?
Methinks I see a host of men:
I marveil quha they be.

She veend it had been hir luvely lord,
As he cam ryding hame:
It was the traitor Edom o' Gordon,
Quha reckt nae sin nor shame.

She had nae sooner buskit hersel,
And putten on hir goun,
Till Edom o' Gordon and his men
Were round about the toun.

They had nae sooner supper sett,
Nae sooner said the grace,
Till Edom o' Gordon and his men
Were light about the place.

The lady ran up to hir tovir head,
Sae fast as she could drie,
To see if by hir fair speeches
She could wi' him agree,

but quhan he see this lady saif
And hir yates all locked fast,
He fell into a rage of wrath,
And his hart was all aghast.

Cum down to me, ze lady gay,
Cum down, cum down to me:
This night sall ye lig within mine armes,
To-morrow my bride sall be.

I winnae cum doun, ze fals Gordon,
I winnae cum doun to thee:
I winnae forsake my ain dear lord,
That is sae far frae me.

Give owre zour house, ze lady fair,
Give owre zour house to me,
Or I sall brenn yoursel therein,
Bot and zour babies three.

I winnae give owre, ze false Gordon
To nae sik traitor as zee;
And if ze brenn my ain dear babes,
My lord sall make ze drie.

But reach my pistol, Glaud, my man,
And charge ze weil my gun;
For, but an I pierce that bluidy butcher
My babes we been undone.

She stude upon hir castle wa,
And let twa bullets flee;
She mist that bluidy butchers hart,
And only raz'd his knee.

Set fire to the house, quo' fals Gordon,
All wood wi' dule and ire:
Fals lady, ze sall rue this deid,
As ze brenn in the fire.

Wae worth, wae worth ze, Jock my man,
I paid ze weil zour fee:
Quhy pow ze out the ground-wa stane,
Lets in the reek to me?

And ein wae worth ze Jock my man,
I paid ze weil zour hire:
Quhy pow ze out the ground-wa stane,
To me lets in the fire?

Ze paid me weil my hire, lady;
Ze paid me weil my fee:
But now Ime Adom o' Gordons man,
Maun either doe or die.

O than bespaik hir little son,
Sat on the nourice' knee:
Sayes, Mither deare, gi owre this house,
For the reek it smithers me.

I wad gie a' my gowd, my childe,
Sae wad I a' my fee,
For ane blast o' the westlin wind
To blaw the reek frae thee.

O then bespaik hir dochter dear,
She was baith jimp and sma:
O row me in a pair o' sheits,
And tow me owre the wa.

They rowd hir in a pair o' sheits,
And towd hir owre the wa:
But on the point of Gordon's speir,
She gat a deadly fa.

O bonnie bonnie was hir mouth,
And cherry were hir cheiks,
And clear, clear was hir zellow hair,
Whereon the reid bluid dreips.

Then wi' his spear he turnd hir owre,
O gin her face was wan!
He sayd Ze are the first that eir
I wisht alive again.

He turn'd hir owre and owre again,
O gin hir skin was whyte!
I might ha spar'd that bonny face
To hae been sum mans delyte.

Busk and boun, my merry men a',
For ill dooms I do guess;
I canna luik in that bonnie face,
As it lyes on the grass.

Thame luiks to freits, my master deir,
Then freits wil follow thame:
Let it neir be said brave Edom o' Gordon
Was daunted by a dame.

102

But quhen the ladye see the fire
Cum flaming ovre hir head,
She wept and kist hir children twain,
Sayd, Bairns, we been but dead.

The Gordon then his bougill blew,
And said, Awa', awa';
This house o' the Rhodes is a' in flame,
I hauld it time to ga'.

O then bespyed hir ain dear lord,
As he cam owre the lee;
He sied his castle all in a blaze
Sa far as he could see.

Then sair, O sair his mind misgave,
And all his hart was wae:
Put on, put on, my wighty men,
Sae fast as ze can gae;

Put on, put on, my wighty men,
Sae fast as ze can drie;
For he that is hindmost of the thrang,
Sall neir get guid o' me.

Than sum they rade, and sum they rin,
Fou fast out-owre the bent;
But eir the foremost could get up,
Baith lady and babes were brent.

He wrang his hands, he rent his hair,
And wept in teenefu' muid:
O traitors, for this cruel deid
Ze sall weip teirs o' bluid.

And after the Gordon he is gane,
Sae fast as he micht drie;
And soon i' the Gordon's foul hartis bluid,
He's wroken his dear ladie.

A comparison of the foregoing with Shenstone's

version will show how much use Percy made of the latter

transcription. Professor Gordon has said that by "dove-

tailing the Miscellany to the correspondence of the two

men we can almost look over their shoulders as they worked

as critics and as editors." [18]   Percy and Shenstone were
indeed "working partners", as this editor states; but it
is interesting to note that Percy did not mention Shenstone's work on the ballad in his notes in the first
edition of the _Reliques_, and equally interesting to remember
that a month before Shenstone's death Percy had written
to Dalrymple suggesting the mingling of "Adam Carre" and
"Edom O' Gordon", a task which Shenstone had apparently
completed. It will be remembered that Percy had difficulties with "Expressions which the Glossaries I have at hand
either wholly omit, or do not explain to my satisfaction".
However it is obvious that he managed the Scotticisms
much better than did Shenstone. His deference to his
friend's taste was considerable; but Percy's own taste was
better than Shenstone's when he reverted to the Foulis text
in 2^1 and 2^2, changing Shenstone's "And to what kind of a
hauld sall we, / My merry men, repair?" back to "And quhat
a hauld sall we draw to / my mirry men and me?" Shenstone's
regrettable descriptive verse 3 Percy left out altogether,
as he did 11, 13 and 25. With these differences, he
accepted the first 33 stanzas of Shenstone's mingled version and limited himself to making slight changes. When
Professor Child reviewed this ballad he was not in agreement
with the taste of either Percy or Shenstone both of whom
retained the five verses found in Foulis which begin with

stanza 26 of Shenstone and 22 of Percy. Child called these

stanzas "deplorable interpolations"[19] and particularly

objected to:

> Then wi' his spear he turnd hir owre,
> O gin her face was wan!
> He sayd Ze are the first that eir
> I wisht alive again.

T.F. Henderson had a different aesthetic judgment, and

stated:

In all ballad literature it would be hard to find anything
more masterly in expression, more vividly graphic or
poignantly pathetic than the five stanzas beginning "They
row'd her in a pair of sheets".[20]

Although the Duchess of Malfi's brother had not much in

common with Captain Carre except wanton, excessive cruelty,

surely the same emotion stirred Ferdinand as suddenly

brimmed over in Carre, when Ferdinand's eyes grew brilliant

with tears at the sight of the fair sister he had murdered:

"Cover her face; mine eyes dazzle: she died young."[21]

Shenstone had not been able to "endure" the ending

of "Edom of Gordon", (the ballad in the Percy folio MS.

had no ending), and he changed it somewhat; but he evident-

ly shared Child's view of the last verse, which Child found

"superior to turning her owr and owr again, and indeed, in

its way, not to be improved".[22]

> Then round & round the waes he went
> Their ashes for to view
> At last he rushd into the Flames
> And bade the world adieu.

This was similar to Foulis's version, with the exception of the third line, where Foulis had, "At last into the flames he flev". Perhaps Shenstone had not been able to endure the triple rhyme, which does not occur elsewhere in the Foulis text.

Percy did not like the note on which Edom of Gordon had ended, although indeed he must have been aware that Scottish ballads are ever more notable for dramatic realism than for satisfactory endings. However, it will be seen that he has concluded his final version with seven stanzas almost entirely re-written from both Foulis and Shenstone, with the husband behaving like an eighteenth-century hero: "He wrang his hands, he rent his hair", but victorious in his vengeance, with his survival or death at the end ~~being~~ a matter of no importance.

Professor Gordon has an interesting interpretation of Percy's editorial methods with regard to this ballad. After discussing Percy's publication, and showing that Percy realized how much both he and Shenstone had added to, or taken from, the Foulis text and the MS. "Adam Carre", he goes on to say:

In view of all this, what did Percy mean hen he ad ed the note 'the orig.' to Shenstone's version in the Miscellany? Shenstone's ballad, as Percy knew, was very different from either of the originals, Foulis or Captain Carre. One could conclude that Percy added the note as an indication that the Miscellany version was <u>his</u> original, the form from which he derived his text for the <u>Reliques</u>. This is

borne out in an unpublished letter of Percy to Sir David
Dalrymple, 11 February 1764, [23] where, in discussing his
alterations to the poem, he makes an almost certain reference to the Miscellany Manuscript. 'I know not how far
you will admit the alterations and enlargements: they
were in some measure pointed out by my late friend Mr.
Shenstone, who left among his papers some hints how and
where he could wish the alterations might be made' (B.M.
Add. 32331, f. 48). But 'the orig.' may only mean that
Percy regarded Edom of Gordon as the 'original' in relation to the derivative Captain Carre.24

Neither of these alternatives is, however, particularly

satisfactory. If Percy regarded Shenstone's as the

original, why did he give credit in the Reliques only to

the Foulis text and "Captain Adam Carre"? It is possible

that he was merely referring to the title as being

derivative. If so, the second alternative is reasonable;

but not otherwise.

It is surprising that the changes Percy made in

the ballad when he issued his second edition of the Reliques

in 1767 have been largely ignored by subsequent editors.

Stanzas 14 and 15 in the edition of 1765 had been taken

from the folio, and are not in the Foulis text:

> But reach my pistol, Glaud my man,
> And charge ze weil my gun;
> For, but an I pierce that bluidy butcher,
> My babes we been undone.
>
> She stude upon hir castle wa,
> And let twa bullets flee:
> She mist that bluidy butchers hart,
> And only raz'd his knee.

It will be seen in Percy's notes in 1765, that he had no

knowledge whatever of the date of the ballad. He placed

it in the feudal age, nd when he came to publish his
second edition he was assailed by the doubt that the
pistols were an anachronism. Therefore in the edition of
1767 the stanzas were changed to read:

> But reach me hether my guid bend-bowe,
> Mine arrows one by one;
> For, but an I pierce that bluidy butcher
> My babes we been undone.
>
> She stude upon hir castle wa',
> And let twa arrows flee:
> She mist that bluidy butcher's hart,
> And only raz'd his knee.

The change is explained by him thus: "The two foregoing
stanzas are improved in this edition by more ancient readings, communicated lately to the publisher. In the former
edition they were evidently modernized . . . ." What
these "ancient readings" were, and how delivered, orally,
or in manuscript form, and by whom they were communicated,
can perhaps be more readily conjectured by us today
than they were by Percy's early readers. That some later
readers demanded more accuracy than Percy was accustomed
to accord is made evident by the notes he appended to the
editions of 1775 and 1794. In them the Gordons still have
their seat in Berwickshire, but this piece of information
is followed by another. "The fact, however, on which the
ballad is founded happened in the north of Scotland (see
below . . .), yet it is but too faithful a specimen of the
violences practised in the feudal times . . . ."

108

It is interesting to note that Percy still maintained the feudal character of the ballad, even though he was then aware of the date of the event, and at the end of the text, "see below", he supplied the information as "recorded in Abp. Spotswood's History of the Church of Scotland . . . . Anno 1571." He added also, "This fact, which had escaped the Editor's notice, was in the most obliging manner pointed out to him, by an ingenious writer who signs his name H.H. (Newcastle, May 9.) in the Gentleman's Magazine for May, 1775." The changes in the ballad itself are important. The bend-bowe and the arrows of stanzas 14 and 15 have been removed and the pistol and bullets restored, with a modest note at the bottom of the page: "These three lines are restored from Foulis's edition, and the folio manuscript which last reads the bullets." An examination of the Foulis text will show that stanzas 14 and 15 were not found in the Foulis version.

David Herd used the version in Percy's edition of 1765, with most of the archaic spelling, and unimportant changes. The Herd version of 1776 was practically a repetition of the first. The proper names, Edom and Gordon, were in upper case letters, an occasional colon had become a comma, and so on. But in its essentials the ballad remained Percy's version. This is not surprising when it is remembered that Herd had not seen Percy's folio

109

MS., and could not know how much of the poem was "the genuine remains of antiquity" and how much was Percy. The transcription which appeared in the collection published in 1791, purporting to be Herd's, was similar to the text in Herd's own collections.

The version printed by Pinkerton in 1781 in Scottish Tragic Ballads had received different treatment. Pinkerton, characteristically, set to right all previous versions, both of ballad and of history, but did not mention that his ballad was copied from Percy's Reliques, 1765. He omitted the seventh stanza, removed the archaisms, and gave his own peculiar version of the Scots dialect, such as "brin" for "brenn", "knie" for "knee", "reik" for "reek", which occasionally is more accurate than Percy's version. Beauty had not come into the ballad, but accuracy came into the notes at one point, when Pinkerton told the history. He called his ballad "Adam o Gordon", and stated: "The genuine subject of this Ballad has long remained in obscurity, though it must have been noted to every peruser of Crawford's Memoirs."[25] He observed that Captain Ker was was sent to summon the Castle of Towie in the Queen's name, which explains why "Captain Car" is the name given in Percy's MS. to Ker of Crawford. He also has an explanation for Rhodes:

of t.e s.ory, .owie. Of w.ich name, I fi.d i. .c
.traloch's map of Aberdeenshire, t.ere were tw.
seats, or castles, in his time, on. u.on the .o..
ot.er upon the Yt.en. The nearest .eat to t.e .
that of .othy, w.ic. fro. wrong information . y.
originally stoo.d in the .alled, t.e mistake .ri.
ly fro. the vicinity of t.eir.git.tion, e.d fr.
have .een corrupted to .odes.[28]

In 1790 .orison followed .inkerton's ve.
text, but slightly changed the notes w.ic. a co..
saying t.at they were .chiefly .ro. .r. .inkerto.
did not .ention Percy's .anuscri.t, nor the .nf.
Rodes, Rhodes and Towie, but gave t.e informatio.
Crawford's .emoirs w.ic. .inkerton had alrea.y .

In the same year, however, .n .ntirely
version of the .alled was publis.ed, surely i. t.
Joseph .itson in his .ncient .o.s .... .li.d. .
.ime of Kin. .enry the Th.rd .. t.e .evolution.
had lon. chafed at .is inability to .ersua.e .er
the precious folio manuscri.t .e seen. .ercy ha.
adamant. But now .itson w.s a.le to tra.scribe .
Car" as he believe. it s..uld be tra.scribed.
it with notes which g.ve information not only on.
but on his own met.ods:

The elegant editor of the .Reliques of .ncient
.oetry" has inserted in t.at coll.ecti.n a .cot.i.
entitled ".dom o. Gordon." printed at .las..w in

the ballad to which the above fragment appears to have be-
longed, the reader is here presented with an entire ancient
copy, the undoubted original of the Scotish ballad, and one
of the few specimens now extant of the genuine proper Old
English Ballad, as composed -- not by a Grub-street author
for the stalls of London, but -- to be chanted up and down
the kingdom by the wandering minstrels of "the North
Countrie." This curiosity is preserved in a miscellaneous
collection in the Cotton Library, marked Vespasian, A. xxv.
. . . The MS. having received numerous alterations or
corrections, all or most of which are evidently for the
better, they are here adopted as part of the text.[27]

Ritson then added that the historical facts are

found both in Archbishop Spotswood's _History_ and _Crawfurd's_

Memoirs. He also added, with his usual asperity, that if

Percy's "old strolling bards" in order to humour their

hearers were ever in the habit of changing the names of the

personages they introduced, such is certainly not the case

with this ballad. The ballad is English, and the Scottish

"Ker" of the original tale has been changed to "car". He

did not explain why the House of Towie has been called

"Crecrynbroghe", nor why Alexander Forbes became the "lord

Hamleton". But he did explain that since Ker was sent by

Sir Adam Gordon to perform the ill deed,

the infamy of the transaction naturally extended to Gordon,
who from the superiority of his station might even be considered as the greater criminal; and as he was, at the same
time, better known, his name was naturally substituted by [28]
the Scotish minstrels for that of his subordinate officer.

Child printed a transcription of the manuscript

discovered by Ritson, mentioning only that Ritson's version

is similar to that of the manuscript, and this is the text

given here:

112

Cotton MS. Vespasin, f. xxv, No. 67, fol. 187, of the
last quarter of the 16th century. [Child noted here that
this was the date given to him, British Museum.]

                    by the

It befell at Martynmas,
  hen wether waxed colde,
Captine Care said to his men,
  we must go take a holde.

     Syck, sike, and to-tore sike,
      and sike na like to die;
    The sikest nighte that euer I aboue,
     God lord haue mercy on me!

'Faille, master, and wether you will,
  And wether ye like it best;'
'To the castle of Crecynbroghe,
  And there we will take our reste!

'I knowe ther is a gay castle,
  Is builded of lyme and stone;
Within their is a gay ladie,
  Her lord is riden and gone.'

The ladie she lend on her castle-walle,
  She loked vpp and doune;
There was she ware of an host of men,
  Come riding to the tone.

'Se yow, my meri men all,
  And se yow what I see?
Yonder I see an host of men,
  I muse who they bee.'

She thought he had ben her wed lord,
  As he come riding home;
Then was it traitur Captine Care
  The lord of Ester-towne.

They wer no soner at supper sett,
  Then after said the grace,
Or Captain Care and all his men
  wer lighte aboute the place.

'Gyue ouer thi howsse, thou lady gay,
  And I will make the a bande;
To-nighte thou shall ly within my armes,
  To-morrowe thou shall ere my lande.'

113

Then bespacke the eldest sonne,
  That was both whitt and redde:
O mother dere, geue ouer your howsse,
  O elles we shal be deade.

'I will not geue ouer my hous,' she saithe,
  'Not for feare of my lyffe;
It shal be talked throughout the land,
  The slughter of a wyffe.

'Fetch me my pestilett,
  And charge me my gonne,
That I may shott at yonder bloddy butcher,
  The lord of Easter-towne.'

Styfly vpon her wall she stoae,
  And lett the pellettes flee;
But then she myst the blody bucher,
  And she slew other three.

'(I will) not geue ouer my hous,' she saithe,
  'Netheir for lord nor lowne;
Not yet for traitour Captaine Care,
  The lord of Easter-towne.

'I desire of Captine Care,
  And all his bloddye band,
That he would saue my eldest sonne,
  The eare of all my lande.'

'Lap him in a shete,' he sayth,
  'And let him downe to me,
And I shall take him in my armes,
  His waran shall I be.'

The captayne sayd unto him selfe:
  Vyth sped, before the rest,
He cut his tonge out of his head,
  His hart out of his brest.

He lapt them in a handkerchef,
  And knet it of knotes three,
And cast them over the castell-wall,
  At that gay ladye.

'Fye vpon the, Captayne Care,
  And all thy bloddy band!
For thou hast slayne my eldest sonne,
  The ayre of all my land.'

11

Then bespake the yorgest sonne,
    That sat on the nurses knee,
Sayth, Mother gay, geue ouer your house;
    It smoldereth me.

'I wold geue my gold,' she saith,
    'And so I volde my ffee,
For a blaste of the westryn wind,
    To dryue the smoke from thee.

'Fy vpon the, John Ferletor
    That euer I paid the hyre!
For thou hast broken my castle-wall,
    And kyndled in the ffyre.'

The lady gate to her close parler,
    The fire fell aboute her heed;
She toke vp her children thre,
    Seth, Babes, ve are all dead.

Then bespake the hye steward,
    That is of hye degree;
Saith, Ladie gay, you are in close,
    Wether ye fighte or flee.

Lord Hamleton dremd in his dream,
    In Caruall where he laye,
Hiss halle vere all of fyre,
    His ladie slyne or daye.

'Busk and bovne, my mery men all,
    Even and go ye vith me;
For I dremd that my heal was on fyre,
    My lady slayne or day.'

He buskt him and bovnd hym,
    And like a worthi knig'te;
And vhen he saw his hall burning,
    His herte wns no dele lighte.

He sett a trumpett till his mouth,
    He blew as it plesd his grace;
Twenty score of Hamlentons
    Was light aboute the place.

'Had I knowne as much yesternighte
    As I do to-daye,
Captaine Care and all his men
    Should not haue gone so quite.

115

'Fye vpon the, Captaine Care,
   And all they blody bande!
Thou hast slayne my lady gay,
   More wurth then all thy lande.

'If thou had ought eny ill will,' he saith,
   'Thou shoulde haue taken my lyfe,
And haue saved my children thre,
   All and my louesome wyffe.'

This version of the ballad is notable for two important differences from all the others. The first is the grim, poignant refrain, meaningless in one sense, and full of life's tragedy in another, with its echo of the haunting, tragic cry of "The Lyke Wake Dirge", "This ae nighte, this ae nighte,/ Every nighte and alle", both of which are surely in the tradition of Dunbar's "Timor mortis conturbat me", and Nashe's beautiful Litany, "I am sick, I must die/ Lord have mercy on me." The other difference is the hideous incident of the eldest son. Here again is the episode of wrapping a child in a sheet and letting him down to the raiders below; but in this ballad Captain Car adds the worst of his iniquities in the wanton, inexplicable torture of the child.

Ritson's version did not give the refrain, but he left unchanged the additional revolting crime, and the curiously inadequate cry of the mother in 18[1], "Fye upon thee captayne care." "The original author" Ritson spoke of had a keen dramatic sense, but the ballad as it stands has no great literary merit. The somewhat anticlimactic last

stanza has an element of realism in it, adding to the
impression already given that the writer was as intent on
telling his tale as it really happened, as in impressing
the events vividly upon his hearers.

Ritson spoke of adopting the changes he had found
written as additions in the manuscript. Child however did
not take cognisance of them, and Ritson did not say which
alterations or amendments he used. The rhythm has become
relatively smooth in Ritson's version, and the rhyme has
occasionally been modernized. The result has not the
polished smoothness of Shenstone's or Percy's texts, and
the rugged irregularities add vigor and originality to the
poem:

Cotton Vespasian	Ritson
3^2 Is builded of lyme and stone	Is build of lyme and stone
3^4 Her lord is riden and gone	Her lord is ryd from hom
4^1 she lend	The ladie lend
5^1 Se yow, my meri men all	Com yow hether, my meri men all
5^2 And se yow what I see	And look what I do see
5^3 Yonder I see	Yonder is ther
5^4 I muse who they bee	I musen who they bee
6^1 her wed lord	her own wed lord
6^2 As he comd	That had comd
8^3 thou shall ly	thoust ly
11^3 at yonder bloddy	at' the' bloady

117

12^1 Styfly upon her wall
    she stode   Sne styfly stod on her
                                 castle-wall

12^3 But then she myst   She myst

12^4 And she slew other three   And sle other three

15^4 His waran shall I be   His waran wyll I be

19^4 It smouldereth me   [The smoke] it smollereth me

21^4 And kyndled in the ffyre   And kyndled in 'it' fyre

23^3 you are in close   you are no 'bote'

24^3 His halle ere all of
    fyre   His halle 'vas' all of fyre

26^2 and like   'All' like

28^4 have gone so quite   have gone so quite[awaye]

      Child used the Cotton Vespasian MS. as his A text.
It gives the tale in entirety, whereas the Percy MS. is but
a fragment. Nevertheless these two versions appear quite
inferior to the Scottish one in tragic horror, awesomeness
and accomplished art. The latter is seldom jejune in
expression as are its English counterparts and indeed has
occasional lines and even stanzas of great felicity.

      The last version to be considered here was published
by Ritson in 1794 in his <u>Scotish Ballads</u>, under the title
"'Adam' of Gordon". The text is from the Foulis chapbook
although Ritson does not give his source. He prefixed it
with the history of the event, as recorded by Archbishop
Spotswood and Crawfurd, and then added:

118

[T]he writer of this ballad, either through ignorance or
design, has made use of Gordons name instead of Kers; and
there is some reason to think the transposition intentional.
A ballad upon this subject, in the English idiom, and
written about the time, which nearly resembles that here
printed, so nearly indeed as to make it evident that one of
them must be an alteration from the other, is still extant;
in which ballad, instead of Adam or Edom o' Gordon, we have
"Captaine Care," who is called "the lord of Easter towne,"
the castle of Rodes is "the castle of Crecrynbroghe," and
the ladys husband is a "lord Hamleton." In other respects
they are so much alike that bishop Percy finding, as he
says, an (apparently incorrect) fragment of the English
ballad in his folio MS. "improved and enlarged" (i.e.
interpolated and corrupted) the Scotish copy "with several
fine stanzas." . . .

It has been usual to intitle this ballad "Edom o'
Gordon;" an error which Sir David Dalrymple, to whom as
bishop Percy says, we are indebted for its publication,
might be led into by the local pronunciation of the lady from
whose memory he gave it.

Ritson's alterations may well have been due to carelessness in proof reading. The version by Foulis was not
consistent in its use of archaisms, neither was Ritson's, but
occasionally Ritson has "z" where Foulis has "y" and _vice
versa_. On one occasion he substituted "Why" for Foulis's
"Quhy". In 21^3 he added an extra foot to even up the
metre. Nevertheless his changes, compared with those made
by Percy, Shenstone and Pinkerton, were slight indeed, and
Carew Hazlitt is justified in asserting that Ritson gained
his reputation for extreme accuracy at a time when accuracy
of any kind or degree was a rare quality. If we had only
the two versions he transcribed, the Scottish and the English, we should not have the worst texts of this ballad,
even though that given by Percy is today the best known and
the one mo   .

Chapter five

. LADY ANNE BOTHWELL'S LAMENT

Following the prevailing practice, I have given
Child's title for this ballad, although the oldest title
is "Lady Anne Bothwel's Balow".

Much has been written about this ballad since it
was first printed in 1711 by James Watson, the Edinburgh
printer, in A Choice Collection of Comic nd Serious Scots
Poems, and considerable controversy has been centred upon
it. Critics have examined it as to nationality, historical
accuracy and literary value, nd several misleading statements have been made. The question of nationality has been
the subject of the most heated discussions, although this
appears to be a matter of a reasonably simple solution.

In this collation simplicity and such brevity as
is consistent with full treatment may best be achieved by
using Watson's text as a starting point, and giving the
manuscript versions in the chronological order in which they
appeared in print.

By entitling the song "Lady Anne Bothwel's Balow"
Watson gave it Scottish nationality; and, for more than one
hundred and fifty years, no ballad editor questioned his
accuracy. Ramsay, Thomson, Percy, Herd, Pinkerton, Johnson,

Ritson, and half a dozen editors of small collections of
songs all left Lady Anne to her Scottish origin. The theme
however is universal: a maiden laments that she has found
too late that men betray. Watson's source for the song is
not known. He printed his songs without notes, except for
a glossary of Scots words; and they are all by Scots
authors, Drummond, Montrose, Aytoun and others who wrote
either in Scots dialect or in English. Since there is no
evidence that Watson ever tried to improve the poetic
quality of his material -- he was a printer, not a poet --
it may be assumed that he printed the ballad as he found it.
Watson's version follows:

Lady Anne Bothwel's Balow.

Balow my Boy, ly still and sleep,
It grieves me sore to hear thee weep;
If thou'll be silent, I'll be glad,
Thy Mourning makes my Heart full sad:
Balow my Boy, thy Mother's Joy,
Thy Father's bred me great Annoy.
Balow, &c.

Balow my Darling, sleep a while,
And when thou wakes, then sweetly smile,
But smile not as thy Father did,
To cozen Maids, nay, God forbid;
But in thy Face his Looks I read,
Who overthrew my Maidenhead.
Balow, &c.

I was too credulous at the first
To grant thee that a Maiden durst;
And in thy Bravery thou did'st vaunt,
That I no Maintenance should want:
Thou swear thou lov'd, thy Mind is moved,
Which since no otherwise has proved.
Balow, &c.

121

When he began to court my Love,
And with his sugar'd Words to move,
His tempting Face and flattering Chear
In time to me did not appear;
But now I see that cruel he
Cares neither for his Babe nor me.
Balow, &c.

I wish I were a Maid again,
From young Men's Flatt'ry I would refrain;
For now unto my Grief I find,
They are all faithless and unkind.
Their tempting Charms, which bred my Harms,
Witness my Babe lyes in my Arms,
Balow, &c.

I take my Fate from best to worse,
That I must needs now be a Nurse,
And lull my young Son in my Lap;
From me, sweet Orphan, take the Pap:
Balow my Boy, thy Mother mild
Shall sing, as from all Bliss exil'd.
Balow, &c.

Balow my Child, weep not for me,
Whose greatest Grief's for wronging thee;
Nor pity her deserved Smart,
Who can blame none but her kind Heart,
For too soon trusting, latest find,
That fairest Tongues have falsest Minds.
Balow, &c.

Balow my Boy, thy Father's dead,
When he the thriftless Son has play'd;
Of Vows and Oaths forgetful, he
Preferr'd the Wars to thee and me:
But now, perhaps, thy Curse and mine,
Makes him eat Acorns with the Swine.
Balow, &c.

Farewell, farewell, thou falsest Youth,
That ever kiss'd a Woman's Mouth;
Let never any after me
Submit unto thy Courtesy;
For if she do, O! cruel thou
Will her abuse, and care not how.
Balow, &c.

122

I wish I were into that Sounds
Where he lies smother'd in his Wounds,
Repeating, as he pants for Air,
My Name, whom once he call'd his Fair:
No Woman is so fiercely set,
But they'll forgive, tho' not forget.
Balow, &c.

Now Peace, my Comfort, curse not him,
Who now in Seas of Grief doth swim,
Perhaps at Death, yea who can tell,
Whether the Judge of Heaven and Hell,
By some predestinate Bastard Lad,
Revenging me, hath struck him dead.
Balow, &c.

If Linnen lacks for my Love's sake,
Then quickly to him would I make
My Smock, once for his Body meet,
And wrap him in that Winding-sheet:
Ay me, how happy had I been,
If he had ne'er been wrapt therein!
Balow, &c.

Balow my Boy, for this I see,
That all this Wailing is for thee;
Thy Griefs are growing to a Sum,
God grant thee Patience when they come,
Born to bewail thy Mother's Shame;
A happless Fate, a Bastard's Name!
Balow, &c.

This version will be referred to here as the A text.

It will be seen that this is a modernized version
and wears all the artless tokens of a broadside. While there
is dramatic pathos, there is also rude bathos; and the moralizing, rare in ballads, is interspersed with Biblical
references. No broadsheet has come to light, however, from
which Watson may have taken his copy. There are no Scotticisms in the poem, except in the title; but this, as has
been pointed out, is not unusual in poems written by Scottish

the Scottish Language (1867) the entry is "Ba low -- a
lullaby. Old Song -- Fr. bas la le loup", which ingenious
fancy was scornfully dismissed by Mackay in A Dictionary of
Lowland Scotch (1888), and replaced by the statement that
the phrase "is derived from the Gaelic ba, the equivalent
of the common English phrase 'bye! bye!' and adjuration
to sleep . . . and laogh, 'darling'." These identification
were ignored by Warrack in Chambers' Scots Dictionary (1952
in his simple explanation, "Ba low, baloo int. a nursery
excl. hush! -- n. a lullaby." The Dictionary of the Older
Scottish Tongue (1937) gives an explanation similar to the
one found in the Scottish National Dictionary (1950):

BA[L]OO, BALO, BALU, BALILLIE int., n., v.

1. int. A word used in hushing a child to sleep . . .

Sc. a. 1724 Lady ... Bothwell's Lament in T.T.
Misc. (1762) 20:
       Balow, my boy, lie still and sleep,
       It grieves me sore to hear thee weep.

2. . . .

Sc. 1721 Ramsay Poems 20.

Syne down on a green Bawk, I trow
    I took a Nap
And soucht a' Night Balillilow
    As sound's a Tap.

3. . . .

Found in O. Sc. (16th and 17th cent.)
Baloue, balow, balulalow.
"Ane sang of the birth of Chirst, with the tune
of Baw lula low," The Gude and Godlie Ballatis
(S.T.S.) 49.

On one point the editors are in agreement -- the
word is in Scots dialect. But even this distinguishing
feature of nationality disappears in the next version of
the song to be published, when it is called "Lady Anne
Bothwel's Lament". Allan Ramsay printed his text in Tea-
Table Miscellany, but whether in 1724 or in 1726 is impossible at this time to ascertain. The text given here
was taken from a microfilm obtained from the National
Library of Scotland of what appears to be the only copy
extant of Tea-Table, 1726, in the possession of Lord
Haddington:

Lady Anne Bothwel's Lament.

Balow, my Boy, ly still and sleep,
It grieves me sore to hear thee weep;
If thou'lt be silent, I'll be glad,
Thy Mourning makes my Heart full sad.
Balow, my Boy, thy Mother's joy,
Thy Father bred me great Annoy.
    Balow, my Boy, ly still and sleep,
    It g[r]ieves me sore to hear thee weep.

Balow, my Darling, sleep a while,
And when thou wak'st then sweetly smile;
But smile not as thy Father did,

12

To cozen Maids, nay, God forbid;
For in thine Eye, his Look I see,
The tempting Look that ruin'd me.
    Balow, my Boy, &c.

When he began to court my Love,
And with his sugar'd Words to move,
His tempting Face and flatt'ring Chear,
In Tire to me did not appear;
But now I see that cruel he
Cares neither for his Babe nor me.
    Balow, my Boy, &c.

Farewel, farewel, thou falsest Youth
That ever kiss'd a Woman's Mouth;
Let never any after me
Submit unto thy Courtesy:
For, if they do, O! cruel thou
Wilt her abuse and care not how.
    Balow, my Boy, &c.

I was too cred'lous at the first,
To yield thee all a Maiden durst;
Thou swore for ever true to prove,
Thy Faith unchang'd, unchang'd thy Love:
But quick as Thought, the Change is wrought,
Thy Love's no more, thy Promise nought.
    Balow, my Boy, &c.

I wish I were a Maid again,
From young Men's flattery I'd refrain;
For now, unto my Grief I find
They all are perjur'd and unkind;
Bewitching Charms bred all my Harms,
Witness my Babe lies in my Arms.
    Balow, my Boy, &c.

I take my Fate from bad to worse,
That I must needs be now a Nurse,
And lull my young Son on my Lap;
From me, sweet Orphan tare the Pan.
Balow, my Child, thy Mother mild
Shall vail, as from all Bliss exil'd
    Balow, my Boy, &c.

Balow, my Boy, weep not for me,
Whose greatest Grief's for wronging thee,
Nor pity her deserved Smart,
Who can blame none but her fond Heart;

For too soon trusting latest finds,
With fairest Tongues are falsest Minds.
      Balow, my Boy, &c.

Balow, my Boy, thy Father's fled,
When he the thriftless Son has play'd;
Of Vows and Oaths forgetful he
Preferr'd the Wars to thee and me.
But now, perhaps, thy Curse and mine
Make him eat Acorns with the Swine.
      Balow, my Boy, &c.

But curse not him, perhaps now he,
Stung with Remorse, is blessing thee:
Perhaps at Death; for who can tell
Whether the Judge of Heaven or Hell,
By some proud Foe has struck the Blow,
And laid the dear Deceiver low.
      Balow, my Boy, &c.

I wish I were into the Bounds
Where he lies smother'd in his Wounds,
Repeating, as he pants for Air,
My Name, whom once he call'd his fair.
No Woman's yet so fiercely set
But she'll forgive, though not forget.
      Balow, my Boy, &c.

If Linnen lacks, for my Love's Sake,
Then quickly to him I would make
My Smock once for his Body meet,
And wrap him in that Winding-Sheet.
Ah me! how happy had I been,
If he had ne'er been wrapt therein.
      Balow, my Boy, &c.

Balow, my Boy, I'll weep for thee;
Too soon, alake, thou'lt weep for me.
Thy Griefs are growing to a Sum,
God grant thee Patience when they come;
Born to sustain thy Mother's Shame,
A hapless Fate, a Bastard's Name.
      Balow, my Boy, ly still and sleep,
      It grieves me sore to hear thee weep.

This version will be referred to as the B text. It also

shows the ballad-monger's art, but has been revised by a

more skilful hand than was A, and there is as little of the

Scottish dialect here as in A. Each text has thirteen stanzas, but they occur in different order:

A - 1, 2, 3, 4, 5, 6, 7, 8, 9, 10, 11, 12, 13

B - 1, 2, 5, 3, 6, 7, 8, 9, 4, 11, 10, 12, 13

A		B	
1^3 thou'll		1^3 thou'lt	
1^6 Father's bred		1^6 Father bred	
1^7 Balow, &c.		1^7 Balow, my Boy, ly still and sleep	
		1^8 It g[r]ieves me sore to hear thee weep.	
2^2 wakes		2^2 wak'st	
2^5 But in thy Face his Looks I read,		2^5 For in thine Eye, his Look I see,	
2^6 Who overthrew my Maiden-head.		2^6 The tempting Look that ruin'd me.	
3^2 To grant thee that		5^2 To yield thee all	
3^3 And in thy Bravery thou did'st vaunt,		5^3 Thou swore for ever true to prove,	
3^4 That I no maintenance should want:		5^4 Thy Faith unchang'd, unchang'd thy Love:	
3^5 Thou swear thou lov'd, thy Mind is moved,		5^5 But quick as Thought, the change is wrought,	
3^6 Which since no otherwise has proved.		5^6 Thy Love's no more, thy Promise nought.	
5^2 I would		6^2 I'd	
5^4 faithless		6^4 perjur'd	
5^5 tempting Charms, which		6^5 Bewitching Charms bred	
5^6 lyes		6^6 lies	
6^1 best		7^1 bad	
6^5 Boy		7^5 Child	
6^6 sing		7^6 wail	
7^1 Child		8^1 Boy	
7^4 kind		8^4 fond	
7^5 find		8^5 finds	
7^6 That fairest Tongues have		8^6 With fairest Tongues are	
8^1 dead		9^1 fled	
8^6 makes		9^6 m ke	

9^1_5 Farewell, farewell 4^1_5 Farewel, farewel
9^6_5 she 4^6_5 they
9^6 Will 4^6 'ilt

10^1 that 11^1 the
10^5 No Woman is 11^5 No Woman's yet
10^6 they'll forgive, tho' 11^6 she'll forgive, though

12^5 Ay 12^5 Ah

13^1 for this I see 13^1 I'll weep for thee
13^2 That all this Wailing is 13^2 Too soon, alake, thou'lt
    for thee;   weep for me.
13^5 bewail 13^5 sustain
13^6 happless 13^6 hapless

This B text was used by Thomson in his *Orpheus
Caledonius*, 1733, with certain interesting changes. The
refrain was no longer the repetition of the first two lines,
but became the reiteration of sounds made in a lullaby,
meaningless but melodious. More important was Thomson's
return to Scots dialect. "Farewel" was changed to "Farweel",
"no more" became "nae mair", and "I wish" was "O gin". Later
in the century this use of Scots dialect in the poem was to
become the accepted mode, but the editors of the *Lark*, 1740
and 1742, printed in London for John Osborne, and the
editors of the *Charmer*, 1752 and 1765, printed in Edinburgh
for J. Yair, reverted to Ramsay's text, in which there were
no Scotticisms, and the refrain was the repetition of the
first two lines. There was one significant change in the
version in the *Charmer*. The song ended at the eleventh
stanza, and the bathos of the ballad-hawker's conclusion
was missing.

In 1765 Thomas Percy published the first edition of
Reliques of Ancient English Poetry, in three volumes, making
no distinction in his title between poems of Scottish and of
English origin. Within the volumes, designations were given,
and "Lady Anne Bothwell's Lament" was sub-titled "A Scottish
Song". Here, for the first time, a source for the ballad was
mentioned, and following his custom, Percy supplied notes,
which he stated frankly were in this case of his own devising.
There appeared to be no doubt in his mind that the song was
Scottish. This is an illuminating ballad in which to observe
Percy's methods. His first transcription, which is found also
in the unpublished edition of 1764, now in the Bodleian
Library, is given here with the notes he appended to it:

Lady Bothwell's Lament,
A Scottish Song

-- refers, I presume, to the affecting story of lady Jean
Gordon, sister to the earl of Huntley. This lady had been
married but six months to James Hepburn earl of Bothwell,
when that nobleman conceived an ambitious design of marrying
his sovereign Mary queen of Scots: to accomplish which,
among other violent measures he sued out a divorce from his
lawful bride, the lady Jean. This suit was driven forward
with such indecent precipitation, that the process was begun
and ended in four days, (in May 1567.) and his wife, who was
a woman of merit, driven from his bed, upon the most trivial
and scandalous pretences. See Robertson. -- History is
silent as to this lady having a child by him, but that might
be accounted for by supposing it dyed.
        After all, perhaps this story is misapplied here,
and indeed it is hardly consistent with the last stanza. In
the Editor's folio MS. whence this song is printed, it is
simply intitled BALOW: and in the copy given by Allan
Ramsey [sic] in his Tea-Table Miscellany, (which contains
many modern additions) it is called, "Lady ANNE Bothwell's
Lament."

130

Balow, my babe, ly stil and sleipe!
It grieves me sair to see thee weipe:
If thoust be silent, Ise be glad,
Thy maining maks my heart ful sad.
Balow, my boy, thy mithers joy,
Thy father breides me great annoy.
　　Balow, my babe, ly stil and sleipe,
　　It grieves me sair to see [thee] weipe.

Whan he began to court my luve,
And with his sugred wordes to muve,
His faynings fals, and flattering cheire
To me that time did nat appeir:
But now I see, most cruell hee
Cares neither for my babe, nor mee.
　　　　Balow, &c.

Ly stil, my darling, sleipe a while,
And whan thou wakest, sweitly smile:
But smile nat, as thy father did,
To cozen maids:　nay, God forbid!
Bot yett I feire, thou wilt gae neire
Thy fatheris hart, and face to beire.
　　　　Balow, &c.

I cannae chuse, but ever wil
Be luving to thy father stil:
Whair-eir he gaes, whair-eir he ryde,
My luve with him maun stil abyde:
In weil or wae, whair-eir he gae,
Mine hart can neire depart him frae.
　　　　Balow, &c.

Bot doe nat, doe nat, prettie mine,
To faynings fals thine hart incline;
Be loyal to thy luver trew,
And nevir change hir for a new;
If gude or faire, of hir hae care,
For womens banning's wonderous sair.
　　　　Balow, &c.

Bairne, sin thy cruel father is gane,
Thy winsome smiles maun eise my paine;
My babe and I'll together live,
He'll comfort me whan cares doe grieve:
My babe and I right saft will ly,
And quite forgeit man's cruelty.
　　　　Balow, &c.

131

Fareweil, fareweil, thou falsest youth,
That evir kist a womans mouth!
I wish all maides be warnd by mee
Nevir to trust mans curtesy;
For if we doe bot chance to bow,
They'le use us than they care nae how.
    Balow, my babe, ly stil, and sleipe,
    It greives me sair to see thee weipe.

Two years later Percy published a second edition of Reliques;

in it many of his ballads and songs, and the notes attached

to them, remained unchanged; but he found reason to disavow

his own presumption, and this song was given with new notes:

The subject of this pathetic ballad the Editor once thought
might possibly relate to the Earl of Lothwell, and his
desertion of his wife, Lady Jean Gordon, to make room for
his marriage with the Queen of Scots: But this opinion he
now believes to be groundless; indeed earl Bothvell's age,
who was upwards of 60 at the time of that marriage, renders
it unlikely that he should be the object of so warm a passion
as this elegy supposes. He has been since informed, that it
entirely refers to a private story: A lady of quality of
the name of BOTHWELL, or rather BOSWELL, having been, together with her child, deserted by her husband or lover,
composed these affecting lines herself; which are here given
from a copy in the Editor's folio MS. compared with another
in Allan Ramsay's Miscellany.

The ballad which follows is a copy of the version of

1765. Obviously Percy found that the comparison with

Ramsay's text called for nothing more on his part than a

change of title back to the one found in Ramsay, and a new

introduction. As frequently happens with Percy, he did not

indicate who informed him; nor, though he stated that the

lady's name was Boswell, did he change the title to suit his

recently acquired information. The footnote appended for 2^2

is so typical of Percy's point of view that it is worth

quoting:

When _sugar_ was first imported into Europe, it was a very
great dainty; and therefore the epithet _sugred_ is used by
all our old writers metaphorically to express extreme and
delicate sweetness . . . . _Sugar_ at present is cheap and
common; and therefore suggests now a coarse and vulgar idea.

The editions of 1775 and 1794 follow the text of 1767, including the notes, verbatim.

In the meantime David Herd, with the avowed intention of giving the readers the songs as he found them, had
begun to publish Scottish songs, with neither additions nor
improvements. He did not always state his sources. His
first volume, published in 1769, contained the song, entitled, as was Percy's, simply "Lady Bothwell's Lament".
But it did not much resemble Percy's transcription. The
refrain was similar to that first set down by Ramsay, but
with "Boy" now changed to "dear". The rest of the poem
followed the text used by Thomson, with a few additional
Scotticisms, for example, "sore" becoming "sair". The poem
contained the thirteen stanzas found in Watson, Ramsay and
Thomson, the order being that of the two last named. Herd
either had an inadequate proof reader; or he still retained
the notion of spelling phonetically, and since _ly_, _lye_ and _lie_
all sound alike, any would do. He used the old spelling of
"ly" from the early versions, in the first stanza, but used
modern spelling in the refrain. Herd published another
collection in 1775, and the ballad was again included.

his possession a manuscript, which contained two ballads,
and like Percy he appended notes. He called his version
"Lady Bothwell's Lament", and it was severely pruned to
four stanzas, of which he said:

These four stanzas appeared to the Editor to be all that are
genuine in this elegy. Many additional ones are to be found
in the common copies, which are rejected as of meaner
execution. In a quarto manuscript in the Editor's possessio
containing a collection of Poems by different hands from the
reign of Queen Elizabeth to the middle of the last century,
when it was apparently written . . . . there are two ballads
as they are there styled, the first The Balow, Allan, the
second Palmer's Balow; this last is that commonly called
Lady Bothwell's Lament, and the three first stanzas in this
edition are taken from it, as is the last from Allan's Balow
They are injudiciously mingled in Ramsay's Edition, and
several stanzas of his own added; a liberty he used much too
often in printing ancient Scotish poems.

                Lady Bothwell's Lament.

        Balow, my babe, lye still and sleip,
        It grieves me sair to see thee weip;
        If thou'lt be silent I'il be glad,
        Thy maining maks my heart full sad;
        Balow my boy, thy mither's joy;
        Thy father breids me great annoy.

        When he began to seik my luve,
        And wi his sucred words to muve;
        His feining fause, and flattering cheir,
        To me that time did nocht appeir;
        But now I see that cruel he
        Cares neither for my babe nor me

134

Lye still, my darling, sleip a while,
And when thou waket sweitly smile;
But smile nae as try father did
To cozen maias: nay, God forbid,
What yet I feir, th t t ou sold leir
Thy father's he rt and face to teir!

Be still, my sad one: spare those teirs,
To weip when thou hast wit and yeirs;
Thy griefs are gathering to a sum,
God gr nt thee patience when they cum;
Born to proclaim a mother's shame,
A father's fall, a bastard's name.

A comparison of Percy's text with that of Pinkerton shows
that the manuscripts resemble each other to a certain
extent. Since Pinkerton does not have stanzas four and
five, his version lacks the felicitous, and most typically
Scottish, line which distinguishes Percy's, "For womens
banning's wonderous stir", and also lacks the moralizing
last stanza. The thread of narrative is now even more
slender than in Percy's version, and his spelling and pronunciation are as determinedly Scottish as even Percy could
wish.

R. Morison, another Scots collector, in 1790 followed
Pinkerton's text, using the same four stanzas, and Pinkerton's spelling. About the same time James Johnson included
the lament in the _Scots Musical Museum_, copying the version
Thomson gave in _Orpheus Caledonius_ sixty years earlier, but
not finding it necessary to become more Scots in the copying.
At this time the English collectors, with one exception, took
their text from Percy, making one or two unimportant changes

in spelling or punctuation ("child" or "boy" remained "bairn", as in Percy).

The one exception was Joseph Ritson, resolute antagonist of both Percy and Pinkerton. He entered the lists with his version of the ballad. At this distance it is impossible, and probably unimportant, to ascertain how many of the stylistic peculiarities in punctuation and spelling in this version were a result of Ritson's carelessness or of his known eccentricities. The notes which follow are taken from his first edition of Scotish Song, 1794. According to Ritson, he had been trying to

discover facts, not to indulge conjecture. Those songs and tunes, therefor, of which intrinsic evidence alone may be supposed to ascertain the age, are left to the genius and judgement of the connoisseur: such for instance as . . . Lady Ann Bothwell s lament.[2]

He added a footnote:

Mr. Tytler classes [this ballad] in his second epoch, that is in the reigns of James IV. and James V. and queen Mary. [But] all his epochs, indeed, are perfectly fanciful and unfounded.[3]

He quoted Pinkerton, saying that Pinkerton "pretends" he has a manuscript in his possession containing two Flowes which "are injudiciously mingled in Ramsay's edition, and several stanzas of his own added." To which Ritson adds:

Part of this is certainly false, and the rest of it probably so. Though some words, and even lines, of Ramsays copy are different from that in the Scots poems, 1706, the number of stanzas is the same in both.[4]

136

While Ritson is inaccurate as to the date of Watson's <u>Collec-tion</u>, he is correct in the other particulars; but it does not seem to have occurred to him that a manuscript might be extant to which Watson, Ramsay and Pinkerton all had access. An examination of Ritson's text, which follows, shows that he took it almost directly from Ramsay, with the only difference being the placing of Ramsay's stanza four. This was nine in Watson, and has become nine again in Ritson. The peculiarities of his punctuation are apparent in the ballad:

Lady Ann Bothwel's 'Lament.'

Balow, my boy, ly still and sleep,
It grieves me sore to hear thee weep:
If 'thou'lt' be silent I'll be glad,
Thy mourning makes my heart full sad.
Balow, my boy, thy mother's joy,
Thy father's bred me great annoy.
Balow, my boy, ly still and sleep,
It grieves me sore to hear thee weep.

Balow, my darling, sleep a while,
And when thou 'wak'st,' then sweetly smile;
But smile not as thy father did,
To cozen maids; nay, God forbid:
But in 'thine eye' his look I see,
'The tempting look that ruin'd me.'
Balow, &c.

When he began to court my love,
And with his sugar'd words to move;
His tempting face and flattering chear
In time to me did not appear;
But now I see that cruel he
Cares neither for his babe nor me.
Balow, &c.

I was too credulous at the first
To grant thee 'all' a maiden durst;
'Thou swore for ever true to prove,
'Thy faith unchang'd, unchang'd thy love;

'But quick as thought the change is wrought,
'Thy love's no more, thy promise nought.'
Balow, &c.

I wish I were a maid again,
From young 'men's' flatt'ry I'd refrain;
For now unto my grief I find,
They 'all are' faithless and unkind,
Their tempting charms 'bred all' my harms,
Witness my babe lyes in my arms.
Balow, &c.

I take my fate from 'bad' to worse,
That I must needs 'be now' a nurse,
And lull my young son in my lap;
From me, sweet orphan, take the pap:
Balow, my boy, thy mother mild
Shall sing, as from all bliss exil'd.
Balow, &c.

Balow, my child, weep not for me,
Whose greatest grief's for wronging thee,
Nor pity her deserved smart,
Who can blame none but her 'fond' heart;
For too soon trusting latest 'finds'
That fairest tongues have falsest minds.
Balow, &c.

Balow, my boy, thy father's 'fled,'
When he the thriftless son has play'd;
Of vows and oaths forgetful, he
Preferr'd the wars to thee and me:
But now, perhaps, thy curse and mine
Makes him eat acorns with the swine.
Balow, &c.

Farewel, farewel, thou falsest youth,
That ever kiss'd a woman's mouth;
Let never any after me
Submit unto thy courtesy;
For if she do, O! cruel thou
'Wilt' her abuse, and care not how.
Balow, &c.

'But curse not him, perhaps now he,
'Stung with remorse, is blessing thee:'
Perhaps at death; 'for' who can tell,
Whether the judge of heaven and hell,
'By some proud foe has struck the blow,
'And laid the dear deceiver low.'
Bal

I wish I were into 'the' bounds
Where he lies smother'd in his wounds,
Repeating, as he pants for air,
My name, whom once he call'd his fair:
No woman is so fiercely set,
But 'she'll' forgive, tho' not forget.
Balow, &c.

If linnen lacks, for my love's sake,
Then quickly to him would I make,
My smock, once for his body meet,
And wrap him in that winding-sheet:
Ay me! how happy had I been,
If he had ne'er been wrapt therein!
Balow, &c.

Balow, my boy, I'll weep for thee,
'Too soon, alake thou'lt weep for me!'
Thy griefs are growing to a sum,
God grant thee patience when they come!
Born to 'sustain,' thy mother's shame;
A hapless fate, a bastard's name!
Balow, &c.

It should be noted here that "Lady Anne's Lament"
did not appear in Evans' <u>Old Ballads, Historical and Narrative, with some of modern date: Now first collected, and
reprinted from rare Copies and MSS.</u>, the first volume of

which was published in 1777 and the last in 1784. It might

be inferred from this that Evans had not at the time seen

the ballad in either a "rare copy or manuscript". Evans'

copy, taken from his <u>Old Ballads</u>, 1810, is given now:

"The New Balow; or, A Wenches Lamentation for the loss of
her sweetheart: he having left her a babe to play with,
being the fruits of her folly."

Balow, my babe, weep not for me,
Whose greatest grief's for wronging thee,
But pity her deserved smart,
Who can blame none but her own kind heart,
For trusting to a flattering friend,
The fairest tongue, the falsest mind.

Balow, my babe, ly still and sleep,
It grieves me sore to hear thee weep:
If thou be still I will be glad,
Thy weeping makes thy mother sad:
Balow, my boy, thy mother's joy,
Thy father wrought me great annoy.

First when he came to court my love,
With sugar'd words he did me move;
His flattering and fained cheer
To me that time did not appear,
But now I see that cruel he,
Cares neither for my babe nor me.

I cannot choose but love him still,
Although that he hath done me ill,
For he hath stolen away my heart,
And from him it cannot depart;
In well or wo, where so he go,
I'll love him though he be my foe.

But peace, my comfort, curse not him,
Who now in seas of grief doth swim,
Perhaps of death: for who can tell
Whether the judge of heaven or hell,
By some predestinated death
Revenging me hath stopt his breath.

If I were near those fatal bounds,
Where he lies groaning in his wounds:
Repeating, as he pants for breath,
Her name that wounds more deep than death,
O then what woman's heart so strong
Would not forget the greatest wrong?

If linen lack for my loves sake
Whom once I loved, then would I take
My smock even from my body meet,
And wrap him in that winding sheet,
Ay me, how happy had I been
If he had ne'er been wrapt therein.

Balow, my babe, spare thou thy tears,
Untill thou come to wit and years,
Thy griefs are gathering to a sum,
Heaven grant thee patience till they come,
A mother's fault, a father's shame,
A hapless state, a bastard's name.

140

Be still, my babe, and sleep a while,
And when thou wake then sweetly smile,
But smile not as thy father did,
To cozen maids: O heaven forbid,
And yet into thy face I see
Thy father dear which tempted me.

Balow, my babe, O follow not
His faithless steps who thee begot,
Nor glory in a maid's disgrace,
For thou art his too much, alas!
And in thy looking eyes I read
Who overthrew my maidenhead.

O if I were a maid again,
All young men's flatteries I'd refrain:
Because unto my grief I find
That they are faithless and unkind,
Their tempting terms have bred my harm,
Bear witness babe lies in my arm.

Balow, my babe, spare yet thy tears,
Untill thou come to wit and years;
Perhaps yet thou may come to be
A courtier by disdaining me:
Poor me, poor me, alas poor me,
My own two eyes have blinded me!

On love and fortune I complain,
On them and on myself also:
But most of all mine own two eyes,
The chiefest workers of my woe,
For they have caused so my smart,
That I must die without a heart.

Balow, my babe, thy father dead
To me the prodigal hath play'd,
Of heaven and earth regardless he
Preferr'd the wars to me and thee.
I doubt that now his cursing mind
Makes him eat acorns with the swine.

Farewell, farewell, most faithless youth,
That ever kist a woman's mouth,
Let never woman after me,
Submit unto the courtesy;
For if she do, O cruel thou
Would wrong them: O! who can tell how?

141

Chambers did not mention Evans' version of the ballad, when he reprinted the lament in The Scottish Ballads. He may not have seen it, or he may not have taken seriously Evans' fifteen stanzas, with their cynical sub-title "A Wenches Lamentation for the loss of her Sweetheart: he having left her a babe to play with, being the fruits of her folly." He believed the ballad to be Scottish, and now, for the first time, testimony was produced as to the identity of Lady Anne and her lover. These notes are of great importance in giving the first clue as to where Watson may have obtained his copy of the ballad, that is from a song sung in Brome's comedy, The Northern Lasse. Chambers quoted the song more or less accurately. The nouns are capitalized in the original, and there are minor spelling differences. The following version, with notes, is taken from Chambers' The Scottish Ballads, 1829:

This pathetic lament, the first edition of which appeared in Watson's Collection . . . and of which Dr Percy has since given a various edition from his folio manuscript, has hitherto been supposed to have been uttered by Lady Jean Gordon . . . and, by another conjecture, has been attributed to a young lady in private life of the name of Boswell. The present editor, by the assistance of a valued antiquarian friend, is enabled now to lay a true and certain history of the heroine before the public.

"Lady Anne Bothwell" was no other than the Honourable Anna Bothwell, daughter of Bothwell, Bishop of Orkney at the Reformation, but who was afterward raised to a temporal peerage, under the title of Lord Holyroodhouse. (He married Queen Mary to the Earl of Bothwell, after the forms of the Catholic Church.) This young lady, who is said to have possessed great beauty, was betrayed into a disgraceful connextion by the Honourable Sir Alexander Erskine, third son

of John, seventh Earl of Mar, (by his lordship's second wife,
Lady Marie Stewart, daughter of Esme, Duke of Lennox.) As
Miss Bothwell's father died in 1593, and as Sir Alexander
had a letter of provision of the abbacy of Cambuskenneth in
1608, there arises a presumption, considering the age of the
parties, that the unhappy circumstance which occasioned the
Lament took place early in the seventeenth century. This,
indeed, is set almost beyond a question by the occurrence of
a poem, apparently the first edition of Miss Bothwell's
Lament, in a publication of the year 1606, "The Northern
Lass or the Nest of Fools."

> Peace, wayward bairn! O cease thy mone:
> Thy far more wayward daddy's gone,
> And never will recalled be,
> By cries of either thee or me:-
>   For should we cry,
>   Until we die,
>   We could not 'scant his cruelty.
>   Ballow, ballow, &c.

> He needs might in himself foresee,
> What thou successively might'st be;
> And could he then, though me forego,
> His infant leave, ere he did know
>   How like the dad
>   Would be the lad
> In time, to make fond maidens glad.
>   Ballow, ballow, &c.

Sir Alexander Erskine was considered the handsomest man of
his age . . . .
        As to the ultimate fate of Miss Bothwell, it is un-
fortunately out of the editor's power to say anything.
That of her faithless lover happens to be better known. He
entered into the French service, and became a colonel. When
the religious troubles broke out in Scotland, Sir Alexander,
disloyal in politics as in love, was prevailed upon by the
Covenanters to undertake the command of one of their regi-
ments. There is, in Lord Hailes' Collection of Letters, one
written, in 1640, by the chief men in that interest to a
person unknown in France, desiring him to intercede with the
Cardinal Richelieu and the King of France, for leave of
absence for Sir Alexander till the end of the campaign then
in hand. Ten days after the date of that letter, the colonel
was blown up, along with the Earl of Haddington, and about
eighty other persons of distinction, in the Castle of Dunglass,
Berwickshire; the powder magazine having been ignited by a
menial boy, out of revenge against his master.. . . .[5]

143

Balow, my boy; lie still and sleip!
It grieves me sair to see thee weip:
If thou'se be silent, I'se be glad;
Thy maining maks my heart full sad.
Balow, my boy, thy mother's joy;
Thy father breids me great anroy.
    Balow, my boy; lie still and sleip!
    It grieves me sair to see thee weip.

When he began to court my luve,
And with his sugred words to muve,
His feignings false and flattering cheir
To me that time did not appeir:
But now I see, most cruel he
Cares neither for his babe nor me.
    Balow, my boy; lie still and sleip!
    It grieves me sair to see thee weip.

Lie still, my darling; sleip a while,
And, when thou wakest, sweetlie smile:
But smile not as thy father did
To cozen maids; nay, God forbid!
But yet I feir, thou wilt gae neir
Thy father's heart and face to beir.
    Balow, my boy; lie still and sleip!
    It grieves me sair to see thee weip.

Farewell, farewell, thou falsest youth,
That ever kist a woman's mouth!
Let nevir any, after me,
Submit unto thy courtesie;
For, if they do, O, cruel thou
Wilt her abuse, and care not how.
    Balow, my boy; lie still and sleip!
    It grieves me sair to see thee weip.

I was too credulous at the first,
To yield thee all a maiden durst;
Thou swore for ever true to prove,
Thy faith unchanged, unchanged thy love;
But, quick as thought, the change is wrought,
Thy love's no more, thy promise noucht.
    Balow, my boy; lie still and sleip!
    It grieves me sair to see thee weip.

Balow, my boy; weep not for me,
Whose greatest grief's for wronging thee;
Nor pity her deserved smart,
Who can blame none but her fond heart.
The too soon trusting, latest finds,
With fairest tongues are falsest minds.

144

Oh, do not, do not, prettie mine,
To feignings false thy heart incline,
Ee loyal to thy lover true,
And never change her for a new.
If good or fair, of her have care;
For women's banning's wondrous sair.
    Ealow, my boy; lie still and sleip!
    It grieves me sair to see thee weip.

Balow, my boy; thy father's fled,
When he the thriftless son has play'd;
Of vows and oaths forgetful, he
Prefers the wars to thee and me.
But now, perhaps, thy curse and ine
Makes him eat acorns with the swine.
    Balow, my toy; lie still and sleip!
    It grieves me sair to heir thee weip.

Yet I can't chuse, but ever will
Be loving to thy father still:
Where'er he gae, where'er he ride,
My luve with him doth still abide:
In weel or wae, where'er he gae,
My heart can ne'er depart him frae.
    Balow, my boy; lie still and sleip!
    It grieves me sair to heir thee weip.

Then curse him not; perhaps now he,
Stung with remorse, is blessing thee:
Perhaps at death; for who can tell,
Whether the judge of heaven or hell,
By some proud foe, has struck the blow,
And laid the dear deceiver low.
    Balow, my boy; lie still and sleip!
    It grieves me sair to heir thee weip.

I wish I were into the bounds
Where he lies smothered in his wounds --
Repeating, as he pants for air,
My name, whom once he called his fair.
No woman's yet so fiercely set,
But she'll forgive, though not forget.
    Balow, my boy; lie still and sleip!
    It grieves me sair to see thee weip.

Balow, my boy! I'll weip for thee;
Too soon, alas, thou'lt weip for me:
Thy griefs are growing to a sum --
God grant thee patience when they come;
Born to sustain thy mother's shame,
A hapless fate, a bastard's name.
    Balow, my boy; lie still and sleip!
    It grieves me sair to see thee weep.

145

In 1853 we learn from Stenhouse's new edition of The
Scots Musical Museum that Charles Kirkpatrick Sharpe was the
"valued antiquarian friend" who gave Chambers his information, and that Sharpe's views were confirmed by passages
"in Father Hay's MS. History of the Holyroodhouse Family"
and "Notes to the Household Book of the Countess of Mar".[6]

Examination of The Northern Lasse reveals that the
heroine was Constance "the northern lasse", a well-born maiden
who spoke with a Scottish accent and who believed, though
erroneously, that she had been seduced by Philip, the hero.
Spurned from him because he mistook her for another Constance,
alias Holdup, "a common whore", she became temporarily un-
hinged and believed she had given birth to a child. Philip
soliloquised, believing he was speaking of Holdup:

Constance! she had a bastard tother day too. What a
mischievous Maw has this she Canibal that gapes for me!
Slight a common Trader, with I know not how many! I marvel
she was left out of Cupids Muster. Sure she brib'd the Ballad-
Maker.[7]

As part of the plot Holdup impersonated the "northern lasse"
and came on to the stage hushing a child and singing the
two verses already quoted--verses which are shortly to be
found in no less than five manuscripts, all dated about the
middle of the seventeenth century.

Continuing with the history of the ballad, we find
that Child in 1857 had accepted the evidence to date and
printed the ballad with notes similar to those of Chambers.[8]

In Brome's comedy of <u>The Northern Lass, or the Nest of Fools</u>, acted in 1632, occur the two following stanzas. They are, perhaps, a part of the original Lament, which certainly has undergone great alterations in its progress down to our times.

Child then gave the two verses from the play which were quoted by Sharpe in <u>The Scots Music l Museum</u>, although Sharpe was in error in attributing them to Constance, the heroine; Holdup, the bawd, sing them. Child continued:

The first professed edition of this piece is in the Third Part of Watson's <u>Collection of Comic and Serious Scots Poems</u>, p. 79; the next in the <u>Tea-Table Miscellany</u>, i. 161. Both of these copies have been modernized, but Ramsay's is the better of the two, and equally authentic. We therefore select Ramsay's, and add to it Percy's, which contains three stanzas not found in the others, and preserves somewhat more of the air of antiquity. There is a version extending to fifteen stanzas, arranged in a very different order, in Evans's Old Ballads, i. 259. Herd, Ritson, &c., have follow-ed Ramsay.[9]

Then followed Ramsay's text, with "Farewel" changed to "Fareweel", and nouns not capitalized. The version Child has given from Percy's <u>Reliques</u> is not an exact copy of any of the many versions examined. Certain words have been arbitrarily anglicized, "mither's" to "mother's", "nat" to "not", while others, "maining" and "maks" have remained in dialect. These changes are important only in showing that when Child pub- twenty-five years later lished his great definitive work/he had radically changed his method of transcribing ballads.

Ritson was long since dead, when, in 1867, largely at the instigation of Professor Child and his colleagues,

Percy's heirs were persuaded to part with the folio long so
jealously guarded. Now, for the first time, Percy could not
only be properly vindicated, but castig ted lso, h d Ritson been available for the purpose. rercy's editors, J.W.
Hales and F.J. Furniv ll, were not of th t st mp, and ere
interested only in imparting the contents of the precious
document, and adding thereto all available inform tion
pertinent to their subject. Each editor performed slightly different part in the transcribing of the manuscripts.
Hales wrote most of the notes on the b ll d:, nd Furniv ll,
among other duties, wrote the section c lled "Forewords",
and here, I, xi, he set down "E lowe (iii. 518) is restored
to its English home."

      The title of the poem is given simply as "E lowe",
and Hales began his notes with the st tement, "This
exquisite song is given in the Reliques from the Folio,
'corrected by another (copy) in Allan R msey's Miscellany'
. . . . On several of these versions Mr Chappell remarks
below:" Then follows Chappell's st tement th t two stanzas
occur in Brome's comedy which are neither in the manuscripts
now printed, nor in R msay. He believes they are an imita-
tion of one of the manuscripts "which h ve an earlier c st
than Brome's lines".

      Hales then enumerated the versions of the b ll d in
manuscript reproduced in the Folio Manuscript, and now given
here:

3. Elizabeth Roger's VIRGINAL BOOK, 1656

The fourth and fifth are Pinkerton's, about which Hales
wrote:

Pinkerton's MS. (temp. Car. I. 1625-49) is now in the
possession of Mr David Laing, and he has kindly compared
for us with Pinkerton's text. The latter he declares to
"utterly worthless. In the MS. the ballad Palmers Blow
consists of six stanzas nearly verbatim with the text you
have given from Gamble's MS., 1649."

He continued his notes as follows: "The ordinary

account of the original personages of this ballad is that

given by Prof. Child in the fourth volume of his English

and Scottish Ballads . . . ." Child's notes, which have

been already given, are then set down, and followed by:

But on this statement Mr. Chappell has been good enough to
draw up, at some trouble, the following:
    "Baloo is a sixteenth-century ballad, not a seven-
teenth. It is alluded to by several of our early dramatic
and the tune is to be found in an early Elizabethan MS.
known as William Ballet's Lute Book . . . as well as in
Morley's Consort Lessons, printed in 1599 . . . . Baloo was
so popular a subject that it was printed as a street ball
with additional stanzas . . . . It has been reprinted in
that form by Evans, in his Old Ballads, Historic and
Narrative, edit. 1810, vol. i. p. 259. The title is 'The
new Baloo; or, A wenches Lamentation for the loss of her
Sweetheart: he having left her a babe to play with, being
the fruits of her folly.' The particular honour of having
been the 'wench' in question was first claimed for 'Lady
Anne Bothwel' in Part iii. of Comic and Serious Scots Poem
published by Watson in Edinburgh in 1713. Since that act
Scotch antiquaries have been very busy in searching into
scandalous history of the Bothwell family, to find out who
of the Lady Annes might have been hushabalooing.
    "May we not release the whole race from this imputa-
tion? The sole authority for the charge is Watson's Collection! -- the same book that ascribes to the unfortunate

Montrose the song of 'My dear and only love, take heed,'
and tacks it as a second part to his 'My dear and only love,
I pray.' Shade of Montrose! how must you be ashamed of
your over-zealous advocate! Let us examine whether the
spirit of 'Lady Anne Bothwel' has more reason to be grateful. Among the stanzas ascribed to her by Watson, are the
two following, which are not to be found in any English
copy:

> I take my fate from best to worse
> That I must needs now be a nurse,
> And lull my young son in my lap.
> From me, sweet orphan, take the pap:
> Balow, my boy, thy mother mild
> Shall sing, as from all bliss exil'd.

In the second we find the inducement supposed to have been
offered by Lady Anne's lover:

> I was too credulous at the first
> To grant thee that a maiden durst,
> And in thy bravery thou didst vaunt
> That I no maintenance should want: (!)
> Thou swear thou lov'd, thy mind is moved,
> Which since no otherwise has proved.

"Comment is unnecessary. Can anyone believe that
such lines were written by or for any lady of rank? Yet
they were copied as Lady Anne's by Allan Ramsay, and polished in his usual style. They have been polished and re-
polished by subsequent editors, but to little avail, for
they remain great blots upon a good English ballad. There
is not a Scotch word, nor even one peculiar to the north of
England, in the whole of Watson's version. The remainder of
Ramsay's copy will be found in the English ballad reprinted
by Evans . . . .
"The acumen of Scotch antiquaries has rarely been
exercised against claims that have been once put forth for
Scotland. Such matters are left for us lazy Sothrons to
find out."

The sad lady and her lover are thus still to seek.

Chappell's footnotes are important as showing the
indifferent, indeed frivolous, nature of his scholarship in
this instance:

Footnote 1. The verse is accordingly altered in R.
Chambers' Scottish Ballads, 1829, p. 135, to

    I was too credulous at the first,
    To yield thee all a maiden durst.
    Thou swore for ever true to prove,
    Thy faith unchanged, unchanged thy love;
    But, quick as thought, the change is wrought,
    Thy love's no more, thy promise nouch'
        Balow, my boy, lie still and sleep!
        It grieves me sair to see thee weip.

Footnote 2. Other portions of the ballad have been treated
in the same way. Even the late Professor V.E. Aytoun, not
content with such changes as "O gin" for "I wish," (to make
it more Scotch) must needs change "With fairest tongues are
falsest minds," into "With fairest hearts are falsest
minds." -- W.C.

It seems unlikely that Chappell should not also have observed, when he noticed Ramsay's "polishing", that Ramsay had given

the stanza exactly as Chambers reproduced it (except for

unimportant spelling differences). And that he should not

have discovered that the change from "O gin" to "I wish" was

made by Thomson a hundred years before Professor Aytoun

transcribed it, and had been copied by Herd in all his

collections. It may be noted also that Chappell has made a

mistake in the number of the page on which Chambers' version

is to be found, and that Chambers spells "sleep" as "sleip",

which gives at least a measure of consistency.

    Before discussing Chappell's arguments, I shall now

transcribe the MS. versions, omitting footnotes not relevant he

The Percy Folio MS.

    Balow my babe, lye still & sleepe!
    itt greeues me sore to see thee weepe.
    balowe my boy, thy mothers ioy,
    th

balow, la-low, la-la-la, ra-row, fa-la, la-la,
la-la, la-la-la, la-low!

When he began to court my loue,
& with his sugred vords me moue,
his ffaynings false & fflattering cheere
to me that time did not appere;
but now I see most cruellye
he cares neither for my babe nor mee.
   Balow &c.

Lye still my darling, sleepe awhile,
& when thou wakest thoule sweetly smile
but smile not as thy father did,
to cozen maids: nay, god forbid!
but yett I ffeare thou wilt goe neere,
thy fathers hart & fface to beare.
   Ballow &c.

I cannott chuse, but euer will
be louing to thy father still;
where-ere he goes, where-ere he ryds,
my loue with him doth still abyde;
in weale or woe, where-ere he goe,
my hart shall neere depart him ffroe.
   Ballow &c.

But doe not, doe not, pretty mine,
to ffaynings false thy hart incline.
be loyall to thy louer true,
& neuer change her ffor a new.
if good or faire, of her haue care,
ffor womens baninge is wonderous sare.
   Ballow &c.

Bearne, by thy face I will be ware;
like Sirens words Ile not come neere;
my babe & I together will liue;
heele comfort me when cares doe greeue;
my babe & I right soft will lye,
& neere respect mans crueltye.
   Ballow &c.

ffarwell, ffarwell, the falsest youth
that euer kist a womans mouth!
I wish all maids be warned by mee,
neere to trust mans curtesye;
for if wee doe but chance to bowe,
theyle vse vs then, they care not how.
   Ballow &c.

The second manuscript version is that taken from
<u>John Gamble's MS. Book, 1649 A.D.</u>, which Hales described as
"a musical MS. belonging to Dr. Rimbault", and reprinted on
pages 516 and 517 of the <u>folio</u>:

Ballowe, my babe, lye still and sleepe,
it grieves me sore to see thee weepe!
when thou art merry, I am glad;
thy weepinge makes my hart full sad.
ballowe, my boy, thy mothers joy,
thy father breedes thee much anoy;
   ballow, ballov, ballow, ballow.

balow my babe, ly still a while;
and when thow wakest, sweetly smile;
butt doe nott smille as ffather did,
to cozen maidens, god fforbid!
butt now I ffear that thou willt leer
thy ffathers fflattringe hartt to bear.
        balow &c.

when hee beegan to court my loue,
with sugred words hee did mee move,
his faineinge fface & fflattringe leares
thatt unto me in time apeares;
butt now I see that creweity
cares neitther ffor my babe nor mee.
        balow &c.

I cannott chose, butt euer will
bee loyall to thy ffather still;
his cuninge hath parlur'd my hartt,
thatt I can noe wales ffram him partt;
in well or woe, wher-eare hee goe,
my hartt shall nere departt him fro.
        balow.

ffarewell! ffarewell the ffalsestt youth
that euer kistt a womans mouth!
lett neuer maide ere after mee
once trust unto thy creuelty!
ffor crewell thou, iff once shee bow,
wiltt her abuse, thou carstt nott how.
        balow &c.

Now by my greifs I uow & sware,
thee and all others to fforbeare;
ile neither kiss, nor cull, nor clapp,
butt lull my younglinge in my lapp.
bee still my hartt, leaue off to moane,
and sleep securely all alone.
                    balor &c.

The third manuscript version was taken by Hales and

Furnivall from Elizabeth Rogers's <u>Virginal Book</u>, Add. MS.

10,337,1658, this having been drawn to their attention by

W. Chappell. In the <u>Folio</u> it is printed side by side with

the previous text:

Baloo my boy lye still and sleepe,
itt grieues me sore to see thee weepe:
Wouldst thou bee quiet ist be as glade,
Thy morninge, makes my sorrow sad:
Lie still my boy, thy mothers Joy,
Thy father Coulde mee great a-noy:
    La loo, Ba loo, la loo, la loo, la loo,
      la loo, la loo,
    Baloo, baloo, Baloo, baloo; Baloo
      Baloo.

When he began to court my loue,
and with his sugard words aid moue
His flattering face and feigned cheare,
To mee that tyme did not appeare,
But now I see, that Cruell hee
Cares nether for my boy, nor mee,
    Baloo baloo.

But thou my darlinge sleepe a while,
and when thou wakest sweetlye smile,
yet smile not as thy father did
To Cusen mads, nay god for-bid
But yett i feare that thou willt heare
Thy fathers face and hart still beare
    Baloo //: //: //:

Now by my griefs I vow and sweare
the and all others to forbeare
I'le neuer kisse nor Cull nor Clapp
but lull my youngling in my lapp,

Cease hrt to moare, leaue of to gro ne,
and sleepe securelye hart a-lone.
     Baloo //: //: //:

No copy of the fourth manuscript was available for
ex mination.

There is sufficient similarity in the first three
MS. versions of the Baloo to warrant our supposing that
they derive from the same source. Since at least five
different copies have been found, it could be assumed that
the ballad was traditional and that accordingly a broadside
had been made from it, a bro dside which, it might be
supposed,had been seen by Watson, and perhaps by Ramsay.
But it is possible that if the broadside existed, it was
English, made from the traditional ballad which had grown
from the lament composed by, or about, Lady Anne Bothwell.

With regard to Chappell's evidence -- unfortunately
he does not specify any of the dramatists in whose work
mention of "Baloo" is made. The question of the tune has
little bearing on the words. Although one may find in
Ramsay's collections poems with the title "The Broom of
Cowdenknowes" this does not mean that the old ballad "The
Broom of Cowdenknowes" is there reproduced. It merely means
that Ramsay has written some verses which will sing well to
the tune called by that name. "Gilderoy" is both the name
of a tune, and the title of a well-known ballad. This is a
fact which causes endless trouble for one who seeks for

ballads in eighteenth-century volumes, and leads collectors
nowadays to ask for a first-line index of ballads, instead
of an index of titles. But Mr. Chappell was too good a
musician, too learned in the lore of Elizabethan music-
makers, not to know this; and he did ill service to Hales
and Furnivall in foisting off his inconclusive evidence upon them. "Baloo was so popular a subject that it was printed as a street ballad, with additional stanzas . . . . It
has been reprinted in that form by Evans, in . . . 1810."
Chappell is here speaking of Evans' printing of the ballad
in his second edition. But there is no other evidence that
a modern broadside existed. I have tried to deduce the
fact that the song was/ a street ballad, but taken from a
version printed at least a hundred years before Evans published his ballads. Chappell's quarrel with the two lines
from Watson's version is purely subjective -- the construc-
tion he put upon the lines is not necessarily that intended
by the writer. With regard to the "Scotch words", the
matter becomes more objective. He stated that in Watson's
version there is not a single Scotticism. But as I have
shown the word "below" is not found in any English dictionary, and is found in all Scots dictionaries. Here the remarks of the anonymous author of the privately reprinted
edition of Watson's Collection are pertinent:

As to the absence of "Scotch" words -- Mr. Chappell is
either not aware of, or he ignores the fact, that the
Scotish p[

instance . . . Sir Robert Aytoun . . . [who] from the nature
of his official connection with the court, must have been
generally resident in London, in which city he died in 1638;
and Mr. Robert Chambers suggests, with some considerable
degree of probability, that he may have been the author of
"Lady Anne Bothwell's Lament," - as it appears in MSS.I and II.
See Songs of Scotland prior to Burns, page 272.

It may here be noted, as a curious coincidence, that
two of Sir Robert Aytoun's Poems "are to be found" in Pinkerton's
MS. (See Scotish Tragic Ballads, 1781, pp. 116-8.) It may also
be mentioned that Richard Brome, who wrote The Northern Lass,
was servant to Ben Johnson, the latter of whom boasted that
"Sir Robert Aytoun loved him dearly."[10]

It would appear therefore that the claim of Chappell

and of Hales and Furnivall as to the English origin of the

lament can be dismissed as not only erroneous but unscholarly,

and regret expressed that the error persists, as for example

in Hugh Walker's statement in Three Centuries of Scottish

Literature, 1893:

Of the older songs which are purely pathetic, two have been
generally singled out as of surpassing excellence. One of
these commonly known as "Lady Anne Bothwell's Lament" has been
proved to be of English origin.[11]

That statement is now contradicted, and it is here claimed for

the lament that it is a Scottish ballad of the seventeenth

century.   In conclusion, however, I should like to express

agreement with the views of Alexander Keith, editor of Gavin

Greig's Last Leaves, 1925:

The internationality of the ballads is so extensive, their
characteristics so similar in every clime where they flourish,
that in examining the ballads of Scotland the researcher might
be investigating those of any country; and arguments drawn
from the traditional minstrelsy of Scotland can with equal
pertinence be found in the balladry of England.[12]

1. The Concise Oxford Dictionary, third ed., gives a somewhat misleading statement: "Simple song, esp. sentimental composition of several verses, each sung to same melody, with accompaniment merely subordinate; poem in short stanzas narrating popular story". But, to quote Hodgart, "ballads are incomplete without music. They cannot achieve their full effect unless they are sung to their own particular tunes, and they cannot be understood historically unless their relationship to music is understood . . . . .[T]heir musical setting adds considerably to their richness and profundity". The Ballads, 46.

The eleventh edition of the Encyclopædia Britannica gives an informative, reasonably concise description of the popular ballad.

2. Gerould, The Ballad of Tradition, 11.

3. Gummere, "Ballads", Cambridge History, II, 395.

4. Hodgart, The Ballads, 31-32.

5. Ibid., 9.

6. Beattie, ed., Roman Ballads, 13.

7. Hodgart, The Ballads, 9.

8. Rustvedt, Ballad Books, 18.

9. Ifor Evans, "Limits of Literary Criticism", Essays and Studies, XVIII, 26.

10. Spiers, Scots Literary Tradition, is cited here also, The Ballads, 167.

11. Motherwell, Minstrelsy, Preface, v - vi.

12. Information taken from Rustvedt, Ballad Criticism,...

13. Ibid., 11.

14. Ibid., 11.

15. Kittredge, biographical notice in Child, English and Scottish Popular Ballads. 1898. I. xx.

157

16.   Hodgart, _The Ballads_, 108.

17.   Henderson, _The Ballad in Literature_, 9.

18.   _Ibid._, 25.

19.   _Ibid._, 24.

20.   Menéndez Pidal, _Poesía popular y poesía tradicional en la literatura española_, 21-23.

21.   Angus McIntosh, _Introduction to a Survey of Scottish Dialects_, Preface, viii.

22.   Quoted by Hecht, in _Songs from Herd_, 25.

Catalogue of an exhibition at the Signet Library, Edinburgh,
1951, "Eighteenth-Century Scotland", iii.

2. Mackail, "Allan Ramsay and the Romantic Revival", *Essays and Studies*, X, 138.

3. Ker, "The Literary Influence of the Middle Ages", *Cambridge History*, X, 221.

4. Woodhouse, "Collins and the Creative Imagination", *Studies in English*, 130.

5. Bernbaum, "The Pre-romantic Movement", *Anthology of Romanticism*, 3.

6. Ramsay, Ever Green, Preface, ix.

7. Morgan, "Modern Makars Scots and English", *Saltire Review*, II, 75.

8. Oliver, "Eighteenth-Century Revival", *Edinburgh Essays*, 80.

9. Mackenzie, Scottish Literature to 1714, 79.

10. Ker, "Literary Influence", X, 226.

11. Ibid., 226.

12. Watson, A Choice Collection, I, no page number.

13. J. Beattie, "Miscellanies" in The Minstrel, I, 5.

14. Dalrymple, Ancient Scottish Poems, Preface, v-vi.

15. Oliver, "Eighteenth-Century Revival", 80.

16. Eliot, "The Spoken Word" in Programme of the London Season of the Arts, 7.

17. Addison, Spectator No. 70.

18. The following is an excerpt from a letter to the editor in the <u>Times Literary Supplement</u>, Dec. 6, 1923, from S.B. Hustvedt:

Sir -- The editing of the "Collection of Old ballads," 1723-25, is commonly ascribed, with reservations, to Ambrose Philips. The ascription and the reservations rest apparently on a note in Lowndes's "bibliographer's Manual of English Literature" (1834). In that work, under the heading "Ballads," sub-title "A Collection of Old Ballads," appears the remark, "This collection is, by Dr. Farmer, ascribed to Ambrose Philips." Lowndes gives no authority for his information; and no further definite evidence connecting Farmer with the Philips tradition seems to have been published . . . .
    One clue of importance turns up, however, in the printed auction catalogue of Dr. Farmer's Library . . . . No. 6, 543 . . . "Phillips's Collection of Old Ballads, 3 vol. <u>plates</u>, 1727".

        The following excerpt is from a letter to the editor in the <u>Times Literary Supplement</u>, Dec. 13, 1923, from M.G. Segar: 'One of the four copies of the "Bibliotheca Farmeriana" in the Bodleian is annotated by Douce. To the entry No. 6543 "Phillips' Collection of Old ballads, 3 vols. <u>plates</u> 1727," he has added the price . . . . Douce thus tacitly corroborates the ascription of the Collection to Ambrose Philips.'

19. [William Wagstaffe], <u>A Comment upon the History of Tom Thumb</u>, anonymous pamphlet. Note taken from comments in <u>Spectator</u>, Everyman edition, 1954, I, 551.

20. Chalmers, <u>Works of Ramsay</u>, I, 17.

21. Gibson, <u>New Light</u>, 88.

                            in his edition 1882-98,
22. In his notes on this ballad /\ Child quotes a version used by Sharpe in his <u>Ballad Book</u>, 1824, which gives to the two heroines "royal kin". He then adds,"the absurd variation of <u>royal kin</u> . . . is printed in <u>The Scots Musical Museum</u>, 1853." I have not been able to obtain a copy of Sharpe, but in <u>The Scots Musical Museum</u>, 1853, this variation does not occur.

23. Woodhouselee, "Remarks", in <u>The Works of Allan Ramsay</u>, ed. Chalmers, I, 51.

24. Oliver, "Eighteenth-Century Revival", 91-92.

26. Ramsay, Ever Green, Preface, xii.

27. "Hardyknute" as Lady   rul-w's composition, is fully discussed in Norv l Clyne's The Romantic Scottish Ballads and the Border Heresy, 1859.

28.   Philips , A Collection of Old Ball s, 1726, Pr face vi.

29. 18th-Century Scottish Books, 85.

30. See Appendix A.

31. Ramsay, Tea-Table, 1727, P. face viii-ix.

32. Oliver, "Eighteenth-Cent ry Revival," 98.

33. Chalmers, Works of Ramsay, I,81.

34. Irving, History of Scottish Poetry, 416.

35. Millar, A Literary History of Scotland, 375-386.

36. Hecht, Songs from Herd, Preface viii.

37. Sherwood, Undercurrents of Influence in English Romantic Poetry, 117.

38. Mackenzie, Scottish Literature to 1714, 1.

39.   Falconer, Correspondence of Percy and Dalrymple, xii.

40. Martin, Ramsay, v.

41.   The following utterances are typical of   rtin's text:

'He may have picked up his small knowledge [of French] in

162

'Crichton [Ramsay's stepfather] with children of his own
could not be expected to provide longer for him. The life
of a farm labourer was not attractive. Miners were treated
almost as serfs . . . . Any person who helped a lad to
escape from such an environment should surely be considered
not as his enemy, but his friend. As for the charge that
Crichton ignored the boy's aspiration to be a painter, we
should note that nowhere in his writings does Ramsay suggest
that he . . . wished to be an artist . . . was it criminal
of his stepfather not to recognise and aid a possible
Angelo? Had Crichton the means to indulge the boy in his
whims? The position of his detractors is ludicrous.'
pp.20-21.

42. Martin, Ramsay, 109.

43. Cecil, "Thomas Gray" in Poets & Story Tellers, 52.

44. Wm. Beattie, Border Ballads, 16.
45. "Edom of Gordon", "Gill Morice", "Young Waters".
46. Murray, Robert and Andrew Foulis and the Glasgow
Press.

47. Foulis's Ballads:

Hardyknute, a fragment of an antient Scots poem.
Robert Foulis, 1745.

Chevy Chace, according to all the Scottish editions,
Robert Foulis, 1747.

Two old historical Scots poems, giving an account
of the Battles of Harlaw and the Reid-squair. Robert
Foulis, 1748.

Hardyknute, a fragment of an antient Scots poem,
Robert Foulis, 1748.

Edom of Gordon; an ancient Scottish Poem. Never
before printed. R. & A. Foulis, 1755.

Gill Morice, an ancient Scottish Poem. 2nd ed.
R. & A. Foulis, 1755. (A first edition has not survived.)

Young Waters, an ancient Scottish Poem. 2nd ed.
R. &A. Foulis, 1755. (A first edition has not survived.)

163

Chapter three

1. Ker, "Literary Influence of the Middle Ages", X, 222.

2. Ibid., 222.

3. Gray, 18th-Century Scottish Books, "Eighteenth-Century Scotland", vi.

4. Macpherson, Ossian, 49-50.

5. Blair, "Critical Dissertation", Ossian, 79.

6. Ibid., 84.

7. Ibid., 84.

8. Ibid., 97.

9. Letter from Shenstone to McGowan, ed. Mallam, 423.

10. Information taken from Neilson's "A Bundle of Ballads", XVIII, 163.

11. [Taken from Deane's]Aspects of Eighteenth Century Nature Poetry, 12. "This is one of the scathing comments of that modern Romantic critic, Raleigh, on the eighteenth-century imitators of Milton."

12. Lovejoy, "The Discrimination of Romanticisms", PMLA, XXXIX, 241.

13. Deane, Aspects of Eighteenth Century Nature Poetry, 25.

14. Ibid., 25.

15. Clawson, Percy's Reliques, 4.

16. Percy, Reliques, 1765, I, ix.

17. The date of the first edition of the Reliques is 1765, but notice must be taken here of an edition in 3 vols. in the Bodleian Library catalogued under the date 1764. These have no title page or preliminary leaves, but on the spine is the legend Percy's Ancient Poetry. These volumes

are in Douce's Collection, and inside one volume Douce has
noted that he bought them at D. Farmer's sale, as supposed
waste, but that they contain some pieces not in the published editions.

18. Ibid., I, ix.

19. Watkin-Jones, "Bishop Percy", *Essays and Studies,* XVIII, 110.

20. Only four volumes have been completed of this
correspondence: Percy and Malone, Percy and Richard Farmer,
Percy and Thomas Warton, Percy and Dalrymple.

21. Johnson, Preface to Shakespeare, lxiii.

22. Boswell, Life of Johnson, V, 360-2.

23. Letter from Shenstone to Percy, ed. Hecht, 6.

24. The Edinburgh Miscellany, 1720, 3.

25. Letter from Percy to Shenstone, ed. Hecht, 8.

26. Ibid., 8.

27. Ibid., 4.

28. Letter from Shenstone to Percy, ed. Mallam, 409.

29. Letter from Percy to Dalrymple, ed. Falconer, 24.

30. Ibid., 58.

31. Ibid., 85.

32. Hecht, Songs from Herd, 21-23.

33. Hodgart, The Ballads, 148.

34. J. Pickford, "Life of Bishop Percy," Bishop Percy's
Folio Manuscript, I, xxxii.

35. Churchill, "Shenstone's Share in the Reliques", *PMLA,* LI,
960.

36. Ritson, "Historical Essay on Scotish Song", *Scotish Song*
lxx-lxxi.

37. Furnivall, "Forewords", Bishop Percy's Folio
Manuscript, I, xxii-xxiii.

38. A fifth volume of The Percy Letters is in progress, consisting of correspondence between Percy and Paton.

39. Hecht, Songs from Herd, 7.

40. Ibid., 8.

41. Henderson, Scottish Vernacular, 339.

42. Scott, Familiar Letters, II, 353-354.

43. Scott, "One Volume More", Poetical Works, 734.

44. Ritson, "Historical Essay on Scotish Song", lxxiv.

45. Burd, Joseph Ritson, 164.

46. Ibid., 163-164.

47. Constable and his Literary Correspondents, I, 414.

48. Hodgart, The Ballads, 148.

49. Burd, Joseph Ritson, 160.

50. Ritson, "Dissertation on Romance and Minstrelsy", I, 70.

51. Taken from the Relicues, ed. Wheatley, I, xiv.

52. Burd, Joseph Ritson, 162.

53. Ibid., 162.

54. Ibid., 159.

55. Ibid., 162.

56. Sir David Dalrymple had now become Lord Hailes.

57. See Appendix II of Percy and Dalrymple Correspondence, ed. Falconer.

58. The Gentleman's Magazine, November, 1784, LIV, 812.

59. Ritson, "Historical Essay on Scotish Song", lxxvi, note.

60. Letter from Pinkerton to Paton, March 31, 1788; taken from _Songs from Herd_, ed. Hecht, 53.

61. J.C. Ewing describes the work of these publishers in an article in _Records of the Glasgow Bibliographical Society_, 1934.

62. Ritson, "Historical Essay on Scotish Song", viii.

63. _Ibid._, 1, note.

64. In 1915 Henry Alfred Burd published _Joseph Ritson, A Critical Biography_.
In 1916 S.B. Hustvedt published _Ballad Criticism_, which has an analysis of Ritson's part in the romantic movement and in eighteenth-century criticism.
In 1938 Bertrand H. Bronson published _Joseph Ritson, scholar-at-arms_.

Chapter four

1. Johnson, Preface to Shakespeare, I, xlviii.

2. Ibid., I, lxi.

3. Letter from Shenstone to Percy, ed. Mallam, 360.

4. Letter from Percy to Shenstone, ed. Hecht, 21.

5. Letter from Shenstone to Percy, ed. Hecht, 24.

6. Shenstone's Miscellany, 154.

7. Ibid., 154. [The punctuation of this excerpt is Gordon's.]

8. Ibid., 122.

9. Ibid., 154. Gordon errs in attributing stanza 24 to
nstone.   It is similar to the corresponding stanza in "Captain Carre
10. Letter from Percy to Dalrymple, ed. Falconer, 13.

11. Ibid., 18-19.

12. Ibid., 26.

13. Ibid., 65-68.

14. Ibid., 68-70.

15. Ibid., 169-170.

16. Ibid., 72.

17. Shenstone's Miscellany, 155.
18. Ibid., xx.

19. Child, The English and Scottish Popular Ballads,
429.

20. Henderson, The Ballad in Literature, 119.

21. Webster, The Duchess of Malfi, Act. VI, Sc. 2.

22. Child, The English and Scottish Popular Ballads,
429.

23. The Percy-Dalrymple correspondence has been blished since Gordon edited the Miscellany.

24. Shenstone's Miscellany, 155.

25. Pinkerton, Select Scotish Ballads, 141.

26. Ibid., 141-142.

27. Ritson, Ancient Songs and Ballads, 180-181.

28. Ibid., 181.

29. Ritson, Scotish Song, II, 17-19.

1. Pinkerton, Select Scottish Ballads, 146.

2. Ritson, "Historical Essay on Scottish Song", cix.

3. Ibid., cix, note.

4. Ibid., cix.

5. Chambers, Scottish Ballads, 118-119.

6. Johnson, Scots Musical Museum, ed. Stenhouse, IV, 204.

7. Brome, The Northern Lasse, Act. I, Sc. IV.

8. Child gives page number 150, but the notes and the ballad are on pages 118-121 of The Scottish Ballads, 1

9. Child, English and Scottish Ballads, IV, 129-131.

10. Anonymously reprinted edition of Watson's Choice Collection, Glasgow, 1869 (only 165 copies made), xxvii.

11. Walker, Three Centuries of Scottish Literature, I, 116.

12. Keith, "Scottish Ballads", Essays and Studies, XII, 100.

APPENDIX A

The first edition at present known to us of Ramsay's
Tea-Table is that now at the Sterling Memorial Library,
Yale University. The title page is as follows:

The Tea-Table Miscellany Edinburgh, Printed by Mr.
Thomas Ruddiman for Allan Ramsay . . . 1723.

A microfilm copy of this volume is in the University of
Toronto Library.

Of the edition of the Tea-Table dated 1724 only one copy
is known, that in the Huntington Library at San Marino,
California. The title page is as follows:

The Tea-Table Miscellany, Edinburgh: Printed by Mr.
Thomas Ruddiman for Allan Ramsay, 1724.

A microfilm copy of this volume is in the University of
Toronto Library.

The next edition known to us contains three volumes in
one, and belongs to Lord Haddington. The title pages in
the order in which they appear in the book, are as follows:

The Tea-Table Miscellany: or, A Collection of Scots Sangs.
Vol. I. Edinburgh: Printed for Mr. Thomas Ruddiman, for
Allan Ramsay, 1727.

The Tea-Table Miscellany: or, A Collection of Scots Sangs.
Volume the Second Edinbrugh: Printed for and sold by
Allan Ramsay . . . . 1726.

The Tea-Table Miscellany: or, A Collection of Celebrated
Songs, Vol. III. Edinburgh: 1727.

A microfilm copy of this volume is in the University of
Toronto Library.

        It should be noted that the edition of 1724
contains only two ballads, "Bessy Bell and Mary Gray", and
"The Gaberlunzie-Man". Here complications arise. In his
bibliography to the edition of English and Scottish Ballads,
1857, Child lists:

"The Tea-Table Miscellany: A Collection of Choice
Songs, Scots and English." Edinburgh. 1724. 4
vols. [Glasgow, R.& A. Foulis. 1768. 2 vols.]

and in the text, on page 124, he gives "Lady Anne Bothwell's Lament, as taken from the Tea-Table Miscellany,
i. 161." Since the microfilm shows the title page without a volume number, it may be presumed that even had
there been two volumes, this was the first. In it page
161 is occupied by "The Gaberlunzie-Man". It may be
imagined that Child saw only a reprint, that of the
Foulis edition of 1768, and perhaps was not fully aware
that every new set of Tea-Table volumes was not identical
with the previous set. Many songs and ballads were added
to editions subsequent to that of 1724, which may be a
satisfactory solution to the question of Child's bibliography and text, but offers no answer to a further problem.
In 1869 a copy of Watson's Choice Collection was published
anonymously, with the notation, "Glasgow. Reprinted for
private circulation. 1869. (Only 165 copies made)."
This volume contains notes on the songs, which were not in
the original volume·Added to the text of "Lady Anne Bothwel's Balow", are several pages of notes on the song,
including the following: "Watson's version consists of
thirteen stanzas, as does also Ramsey's which appeared in
the Tea-Table Miscellany, 1724." It is obvious that for
the time being the question of what Tea-Table of 1724
consisted, must be left unresolved.

side. Printed ballads did not assume the form of chapbooks until after the first decade of the eighteenth
century. These broadsides were extremely popular. In
his <u>Popular Music of the ancien time</u>, I, 106, Chappell
notes that "seven hundred and ninety-six ballads left for
entry at the Stationers' Hall remained in the cupboard of
the Council Chamber of the Company at the end of the year
1560, to be transferred to the new Wardens, and only forty-
four books." They were not always approved however.
Wheatley notes sixteenth-century opinion of ballads,
"the new literature that was rising up like a mushroom",
in the foreword to his edition of the Pepys. He shows
that this opinion does not tend to improve with the passage
of time. On page xxxvii, he notes:

[W]e find the following character in the curious little
book, entitled <u>Whimzies, or a New Cast of Characters</u> (1631)
"A ballad monger is the ignominious nickname of a penurious
poet, of whom he partakes in nothing but in povertie. He
has a singular gift of imagination, for he can descant on
a man's execution long before his confession. Nor comes
his invention far short of his imagination. For art of
truer relations, for a neede, he can finde you out a
Sussex dragon, some sea or inland monster, drawne out by
some Shoe-lane man in a Gorgon-like feature, to enforce more
horror in the beholder,"!

Wheatley notes that in December 1648 the Provost Marshal
was given power to seize all ballad singers, and that by
1653 there were no more entries of ballads at Stationers'
Hall. Strangely enough Oliver Cromwell removed the ban;
ballads were sung again, and after the Restoration even the
courtier poets wrote street ballads. The fashion changed
again. It was realized soon that ballad singers had too
too much liberty to write and sing as they pleased. They
were ordered to procure licenses both to sing the ballads
and to sell them. By 1710 ballad singing was so much out
of favour with the authorities that the singing of ballads
about the streets was denounced as a common nuisance.
Addison's praise was not sufficient to make ballads
respectable.

A letter in <u>The London Magazine</u> of March 1725,
reprinted from <u>The Grub Street Journal</u> of February of the
same year, gives a not isolated point of view:

'The scandalous Practice of _Ballad-singing_ is a continual
Nursery for Idlers, Whores, and Pickpockets; a School for
Scandal, Smut and Debauchery . . . and ought to be entirely
suppressed; or at least reduced to proper Restrictions.'

Percy is later in the century to bring forward the idea
that ballad singers were once of an honourable and highly
respected fraternity, but in 1735 _The London Magazine_ takes
no cognizance of their ancestry in replying to the
complaint:

'Whether or not the ballads come under the stamp act, there
is no question that the law regards ballad-singers as
vagrants who may be punished by any magistrate. If news-
papers pay duty, why should not ballads? Children who are
permitted to be familiar with footmen and other domestics
hear ballads of "How the young Squire, Master's eldest Son,
fell in love with the Chamber-maid . . ." By such means#
young master and miss are taught to love to their hurt.'

_The London Magazine or Gentleman's Monthly
Intelligencer._ London, March 1735. 155-160.

Addison, Joseph. The Spectator. London, 1711. Nos. 70
    and 74.

Aungervyle Society Reprints, No. 5. "A Garland of Old
    Historical Ballads". Edinburgh: Privately printed
    for the Aungervyle Society, 1881-82.

Boswell, James. Life of Johnson. Ed. George Birbeck
    Hill. 6 vols. Oxford: Clarendon Press, 1934.

Brome, Richard. The Northern Lasse, or, A Nest of Fools.
    London, 1632.

Callander, John, ed. Two Ancient Scottish Poems: The
    Gaberlunzie-Man, and Christ's Kirk on the Green.
    Edinburgh, 1782.

Campbell, Alexander. An Introduction to the History of
    Poetry in Scotland . . . to return with a conversation
    on Scotish Song . . . to which are subjoined Songs of
    the Lowlands of Scotland. Edinburgh, 1798.

Caw, G., ed. The Poetical Museum. Hawick, 1784.

Collins, William. Poetical Poems. Ed. . . . ranson.
    Boston: Ginn, 1898.

The Complaynt of Scotland, 1549. Reprinted, Edinburgh,
    1801. Ed. John Leyden.

[Constable, Archibald] Archibald Constable and his
    Literary Correspondents. 3 vols. Edinburgh, 1783.

Dalrymple, David (Lord Hailes), ed. Ancient Scottish
    Poems, published from the MS. of George Bannatyne,
    MDLXVIII. Edinburgh, 1770.

Durfey, Thomas, ed. Wit and Mirth: or Pills to Purge
    Melancholy. 6 vols. London, 1719-1720.

Edinburgh Assembly: by various Hands. Edinburgh, 17__.

Evans, Thomas, ed. Old Ballads, Historical and Narrati
with some of modern date. 4 vols. London, 1777-84

--------. Old Ballads. A new, revised and considerabl
enlarged collection. London, 1810.

Foulis, Robert and Andrew, eds. Chapbooks. Glasgow,
1745-55.

The Gentleman's Magazine. London, November, 1784, LIV
2nd part, 812-814. [Unsigned, open letter from Lit
to John Pinkerton].

Gordon, Ian A., ed. Shenstone's Miscellany, 1759-63.
Oxford: Clarendon Press, 1952.

Gray, Thomas. The Poems of Gray and Collins. Ed.
Austen Poole. London: Oxford University Press,
1937.

Gude and Godlie Ballatis. Reprinted by Scottish Text
Society. Edinburgh: Blackwood, 1897.

Hailes, Lord. See Dalrymple, David.

Hales, J.W. and F.J. Furnivall, eds. Bishop Percy's
Folio Manuscript, Ballads and Romances. London:
Trubner, 1867.

Hecht, Hans, ed. Thomas Percy und William Shenstone.
Briefwechsel aus der Entstehungszeit der Reliques
Quellen und Forschungen. Strassburg: Trubner, 1

Herd, David, ed. The ancient and modern Scots Songs,
Heroic Ballads, &c. Edinburgh, 1769.

--------. Ancient and Modern Scottish Songs, heroic
Ballads, &c. 2 vols. 2nd ed. Edinburgh, 1776.

--------. Antient and Modern Scotish Songs, Heroic
Ballads, &c. Edinburgh, 1791.
(This edition was not edited by Herd, nor
authorized by him. However it contains much
of his material, and additional selections, an
is generally referred to as his third edtion.

Home, John. Douglas. A Tragedy. London, 1791.

Edinburgh, 1787-8..

Johnson, ..n, ed. The ..l ys of 1111.
    London, 1766. [Preface].

Leyden, John. See ..mpl yrt of .cotla

The London Magazine or Gentleman's .on
    London, March, 1765. 165-166.

'acph rson, James. ..oe s of ..ssian, t
    a .reliminary .iscourse, .n. isse
    and Poems of Ossian. London, 1825

Maidment, James, ed. Letters from Jos
    to .r. .e rge ..ton. .dinburgh, 1

Morison, R., ed. ..elect ..ollection
    Ballads. 4 vols. .erth, 1790.

.icholson, C., ed. ..cotish ..llads n
    1796.

..rpheus Caledonius. See Tho son, 111

.ennant, Thomas. A Tour in .cotland a
    Hebrides in 177.. .ondon, 1774-7

.ercy, Thomas, ed. .isho .ercy's Fol
    see Hales, J. . and .urnivall. F.T.

--------. .ercy's Ancient .oetry.   3
    1764.

--------. Reli-ues of ..cient E.lish
    London, 1765.

--------, --------. 3 vols. ..nd ed.

--------, --------. 3 vols. 3rd ed.

--------, --------. 3 vols. 4th ed.

The .ercy Letters. .en. eds. ..vid .l..
    ..eanth .rooks. [..ton .ouge]: .o
    Univ.rsity .ress, 1944-

    1. The .orres.ondence of .ho..s ..
        ..lone. .d. .rthur .illotson,

II. <u>The Correspondence of Thomas Percy and Richard Farmer</u>. Ed. Cleanth Brooks, 1946.

III. <u>The Correspondence of Thomas Percy and Thomas Warton</u>. Ed. M.G. Robinson and Leah Dennis, 1951.

IV. <u>The Correspondence of Thomas Percy and David Dalrymple, Lord Hailes</u>. Ed. A.F. Falconer, 1954.

Philips, Ambrose, ed. <u>A Collection of Old Ballads</u>. 2 vol London, 1723.

————. ————. London, 1725.

————. ————. London, 1726.

————. ————. London, 1727.

————. ————. London, 1738.

Pinkerton, John, ed. <u>Scotish Tragic Ballads</u>. London, 17

————. <u>Select Scotish Ballads</u>. London, 1783.

· · · · · · · · · add here item Pinkerton, John from p. 153.

Ramsay, Allan. <u>Allan Ramsay's Works</u>. Edinburgh, 1720.

————. <u>Scots Songs</u>. Edinburgh, 1720.

————. <u>Ramsay's Poems</u>. Edinburgh, 1721.

————. <u>The Tea-Table Miscellany</u>. Edinburgh, 1723.

————. ————. Edinburgh, 1724.

————. <u>The Ever Green, being a collection of Scots Poems, wrote by the Ingenious before 1600</u>. 2 vols. Edinburgh, 1724.

————. <u>The Tea-Table Miscellany: or, A Collection of Scots Songs</u>. 3 volumes in one, each with a different title page. Edinburgh, 1726-27.

————. <u>A New Miscellany of Scots Songs</u>. London, 1727.

————. <u>The Tea-Table Miscellany: or, Allan Ramsay's Collection of Scots Songs</u>. London, 1730.

————. <u>The Tea-Table Miscellany, or, a Collection of Choice Songs, Scots and English</u>. London, 1734.

Ramsay, Allan. The Tea-Table Miscellany, or, a Collection
    of Choice Songs, Scots and English. Edinburgh, 1760.

----------. The Ever-Green, being Collection of Scots
    Poems wrote by the Ingenious before 1600. Edinburgh,
    1761.

----------. The Tea-Table Miscellany: A Collection of
    Choice Songs, Scots and English. Glasgow: Foulis,
    1768.

----------. The Tea-Table Miscellany. Glasgow, 1782.

----------. ----------. Reprinted from the fourteenth edition.
    Glasgow: Forrester, 1876.

Ritson, Joseph, ed. Ancient Songs and Ballads, from the
    time of King Henry the Third to the Revolution.
    London, 1790.

----------. "Dissertation on Romance and Minstrelsy".
    Ancient Engleish Metrical Romancees. 2 vols. London,
    1802.

----------. Scotish Song. 2 vols. London, 1794.

----------. The Caledonian Muse, A chronological selection
    of Scotish Poetry from the earliest times. London,
    1785. (Not issued until 1821.)

----------. The Northumberland Garland. Newcastle, 1792.

----------. The Northumberland Garland, or Newcastle Nightin-
    gale. Newcastle, 1793.

----------. A Select Collection of English Songs, with their
    Original Airs. 3 vols. London, 1783.

----------. The Northern Garland. Stockton, 1784.

----------. Ancient Songs and Ballads, from the Reign of King
    Henry the Second to the Revolution. 2 vols. London, 1829

Scott, Tom. Seeven Poems O Maister Francis Villon made owre
    intil Scots. Tunbridge Wells: Pound Press, 1953.

Scott, Sir Walter. Familiar Letters of Sir Walter Scott.
    2 vols. Edinburgh: Douglas, 1894.

----------. ----------.
    Edin

Scott, Sir Walter. The Antiquary. 3 vols. Edinburgh, 1816.

——————. "One Volume More", Poetical Works. Ed. Robt. Ford. London: Collins. [n.d.]

Shenstone, William. The Letters of William Shenstone. Ed. Duncan Mallam. Minneapolis: University of Minnesota Press, 1939.

——————. The Letters of William Shenstone. Ed. Marjorie Williams. Oxford: Blackwell, 1939.

Smith, Sidney Goodsir. So Late into the Night. Edinbur: Oliver, Boyd, 1952.

Temple, Sir William, Bt. The Works of Sir William Temple, Bt. 4 vols. London, 1757.

Thomson, George, ed. The Melodies of Scotland, &c. 6 vols. Edinburgh, 1793-1841.

Thomson, James. The Poetical Works of James Thomson. Edinburgh, 1853.

Thomson, William, ed. Orpheus Caledonius, or A Collection of the best Scotch Songs set to Musick by W. Thomson. London, 1725.

——————. ——————. The Second edition. London, 1733.

Tytler, William. "A Dissertation on the Scottish Music prefixed to A Selection of the most favourite Scots Songs, chiefly pastoral. London, 1790-92.

Wagstaffe, William, Dr. A Comment upon the History of Tom Thumb, anonymous pamphlet. London, 1711. As quoted in Addison's Spectator, Everyman edition, 1954, I.

Watson, James, ed. A Choice Collection of Comic and Serious Scots Poems both Ancient and Modern, By Several Hands. Edinburgh, 1706-11.

——————. ——————. Reprinted for private circulation. Glasgow, 1869.

Beattie, James. "Miscellanies by James Beattie",
The Minstrel. 2 vols. London, 1807. [Notes].

Beattie, William, ed. Border Ballads. Edinburgh:
Penguin Books, 195?. [Introduction].

Bernbaum, Ernest, ed. English Poets of the Eighteenth
Century. New York: Scribners, 1918. [Intro-
duction].

--------. Anthology of Romanticism. New York: no id
Press, 1948. [Introduction].

Bronson, Bertrand H. Joseph Ritson, scholar-at-arms.
Berkeley: University of California Press, 1938.

Burd, Henry Alfred. Joseph Ritson, A Critical Biography
reprinted from The University of Illinois Studies
Language and Literature. Illinois, 1916.

Burns, Robert. The Poetry of Robert Burns. Ed. W.E.
and T.F. Henderson. London: Caxton, 1896. [Intro
duction].

Case, A.E. A Bibliography of English Poetical Miscell
1521-1750. Oxford: Oxford University Press, 1935

Cecil, Lord David. "Thomas Gray", Poets and Story-T
A Book of Critical Essays. New York: Macmillan.
1949. 47-73.

Chalmers, George, ed. The Poems of Allen Ramsay. 2 v
London, 1850.

--------. The Works of Allan Ramsay. 2 vols. London
1851. [Essays and notes].

Chambers, Robert, ed. The Scottish Ballads. Edinburgh,
1829. [Notes].

--------. The Songs of Scotland prior to Burns.
Edinburgh, 1862. [Notes].

Chappel., ..., ed. A Collection of N tion l En lish
    Airs. 2 vols. London, 1838-40. [Notes].

Child F.J., ed. English and Scottish Ballads. 8 vols.
    Boston: Little, Brown, 1857-59.

————, ————. 8 vols. 2nd ed. Boston: Little,
    Brown, 1864.

————. The En lish and Scottish Popular B llads.
    5 vols. Boston: Houghton, Mifflin, 1882-98.
        [The above edition was also issued as ten volumes,
        but indexed as five. The University of Toronto
        library has had this set rebound as 1 , 1 , 2 ,
        2 and so on].

Clyne, Norval. The Romantic Scottish Ballads and the
    Wardlaw Heresy. Aberdeen, 1859.

Cowley, J.D. Bibliographical Description and
    Cataloguing. London: Grafton, 1939.

Deane, C.V. Aspects of Eighteenth Century Nature
    Poetry. Oxford: Blackwood, 1935.

Dick, J.C., ed. The Songs of Robert Burns. London:
    Frowde, 1903. [Notes].

Eliot, T... "The Metaphysical Poets", Selected Essays.
    London: Faber, 1932, **281-291.**

Frank, Joseph, ed. The Letters of Joseph Ritson, Esq..
    Edited chiefly from originals in the possession
    of his nephew. To which is prefixed a Memoir
    of the Author by Sir Harris Nicolas. 2 vols.
    London, 1833. [Notes].

Gerould, G.H. The Ballad of Tradition. Oxford:
    Clarendon Press, 1932.

Gibson, Andrew. New Light on ... Burns. Edinburgh:
    Brown, 1927.

Gordon, Ian A., ed. Shenstone's Miscellany, 1759-63.
    Oxford: Clarendon Press, 1952. [Introduction and
    notes].

Graham, Henry Grey. The Social Life of Scotland in
the Eighteenth Century. London: Black, 1937.

Greig, Gavin. See Keith, A. Last Leaves . . . .

Gummere, F.B. The Popular Ballad. Boston:
Houghton, Mifflin, 1907.

Hazlitt, W. Carew, ed. Remains of the Early Popular
Poetry. London: Russell Smith, 1864.[Notes].

Hecht, Hans, ed. Songs from David Herd's Manuscripts.
Edinburgh: May, 1904. [Introduction and notes].

Henderson, T.F. The Ballad in Literature. Cambridge:
University Press, 1912.

———. Scottish Vernacular Literature. 2nd ed.
Edinburgh: Grant, 1910.

Hodgart, M.J.C. The Ballads. London: Hutchinson's
University Library, 1950.

Hume, David. Essays, moral, political and literary.
Ed. T.H. Green and T.H. Grose. London: Longmans,
Green, 1898.

Hustvedt, Sigurd Bernhard. Ballad Books and Ballad
Men. Cambridge, Mass: Harvard University Press,
1930.

———. Ballad Criticism in Scandinavia and Great
Britain during the Eighteenth Century. New York:
American-Scandinavian Foundation, 1916.

Irving, David. The History of Scottish Poetry.
Edinburgh: Edmonston, Douglas, 1861.

Jamieson, Robert, ed. Popular Ballads and Songs.
Edinburgh, 1806. [Notes].

Johnson, James, ed. The Scots Musical Museum. Now
accompanied with...notes . . . by Wm. Stenhouse.
4 vols. Edinburgh, 1853. [Notes].

Keith, A., ed. Last Leaves of Traditional Ballads and
Ballad Airs. Collected in Aberdeenshire by the
late Gavin Greig. Aberdeen, 1925. [Notes].

McIntosh, Angus. An Introduction to a Survey of Scottish
Dialects. Edinburgh: Published for University of
Edinburgh by Nelson. 1952.

--------, ed. ...ttish ......: ublis.. for t..
....ti... ...i.... ....: ...., ...,
1948.

...dm..t, J..es, ed. ...tti.. ...l'.d. ....,
.istorical .nd .r.dition.ry. . v.ls. .di...gh,
1868. [.otes].

..rtin, .urns. .l.n ... X. ..tuty of .is .i.. n..
....orks. .... ..id.., ...: ..rv.rd U.i..s'ty .r..
19.1.

..rtin, .urns, .nd ... .liver, ed. ....s of .ll .n
....s... ....urgh: ...ckwood, 1948-...

.illar, John ..pburn. ...lit. .r ..l... .r of ...ill n...
...on: ..in, 18...

.otherwell, .illiam. ...ntrol.y: ..ient .nd ....r.
Glas..ow: .ylie, 18.7. [.....duction].

.ercy, Thom.s, ed. .oll....s of ...ient ....lish ...t..
.d. ....athley. ...don: ..C.....win, 18.9.
[.otes].

[..bert..n, John, ed. ...h..'. ..ti.. ....t.. .f
the ...col...ti.... .f ...h ...... .f ......
.c...l.ss ...ses writ... .... .t 1. ill
1658. . v.ls. ....n, 1785.]   Transfer to p.

..ound, Louisa. ...tic .r...... 1 .. ... t.... 2.d. .... .ork:
M.cmill.n, 19.1.

.herw..d, ...r.t. ...ti.. ..it... .f ... .t..
..nglish .om.ntic ...try. .... J ...: ....n
U.iv..sity .ress, 19.7.

..irley, G... ..rnfri.s .int..s i. ... .i..t.... t...t
.entury .it. ...dlists of th.ir ..rks. ...d .oc....
.umri.., ...r.o., 1964.

.ping..n, J. ..., ed. .r ..l.ls .... .i.. ....
...ient and .o..rn ..d .... i. ...etry. ...ford:
..ler.nd.. .r.ss, 1869. [.ntrod...ti..].

Taylor, Archer. "Edward" and "Sven i Rosengard". A study in the dissemination of the ballad. Chicago: University of Chicago Press, 1931.

Veitch, John. The History and Poetry of the Scottish Border. 2 vols. Edinburgh: Blackwood, 1893.

Walker, Hugh. Three Centuries of Scottish Literature. 2 vols. Glasgow: Maclehose, 1893.

Warton, Thomas. History of English Poetry. 3 vols. Oxford, 1774-81.

Wheatley, H.B. See/Reliques of Ancient English Poetry, 1889.
Percy,

Williams, Marjorie. William Shenstone. Birmingham: Cornish, 1935.

Woodhouse, A.S.P. "Collins and the Creative Imagination" in Studies in English by Members of University College. Collected by M.W. Wallace. Toronto: University of Toronto Press, 1931.

Woodhouselee, Lord. "Remarks on the Genius and Writings of Allan Ramsay", in The Works of Allan Ramsay. Ed. George Chalmers. 2 vols. London, 1851.

II

ARTICLES

eyne, Thomas. "David Herd", Dictionary of National Biography. XXVI (1891), 236-7.

hambers' Cyclopedia of Literature. vols. London, (1903), II, 797.

hurchill, Irving L. "William Shenstone's Share in the Preparation of Percy's Reliques", Publication of the Modern Language Association. LI (Dec. 1936), 960-974.

lawson, .B. "Percy's Reliques of Ancient English Poetry". n.d. 11 pp. Reprint of article in eport of the Ontario Educational Association, 1913.

liot, T... "The Spoken Word", article in Programme, London Season of the Arts, 1951. London: Lund, Humphries, 1951, 6-9.

vens, . Ifor. "The Limits of Literary Criticism", Essays and Studies by Members of the English Association. Oxford: Clarendon Press, XXIII (1935), 24-52.

wing, J.C. "Brash and Reid", Records of the Glasgow Bibliographical Society. Glasgow: Maclehose, 1934, 20 pp.

rey, Sir Alexander, ed. 18th Century Scottish Books. Catalogue of exhibition at Signet Library, Edinburgh, 1951. Edinburgh: Cambridge University Press, 1951. x + 187 pp.

ummere, ... "Ballads", Cambridge History of English Literature. II(1908) 395-418.

ustvedt, .B. Letter to Times Literary Supplement, London, Dec. 6, 1923.

eith, Alexander. "Scottish Ballads; Their Evidence of Au
by Ke
Clare

Ker, W.P. "The Literary Influence of the Middle Ages",
    Cambridge History of English Literature. X (1934),
    217-241.

Lovejoy, A.O. "The Discrimination of Romanticisms",
    Publication of the Modern Language Association.
    XXIX (1924), 229-253.

Mackail, J.W. "Allan Ramsay and the Romantic
    Revival", Essays and Studies by Members of the
    English Association. X (1924), 137-144.

Morgan, Edwin. "Modern Makars - Scots and English",
    Saltire Review. Edinburgh: Saltire Society,
    II (Aug. 1954), 75-81.

Murrey, David. Robert and Andrew Foulis and the
    Glasgow Press. Glasgow: Maclehose, 1913, 144 pp.

-----------. Some Letters of Robert Foulis. Reprinted
    from the Scottish Historical Review. Glasgow:
    Maclehose, 1917, 72 pp.

Neilson, George. "A Bundle of Ballads", Essays and
    Studies by Members of the English Association.
    VII (1921), 108-142.

Oliver, John W. "The Eighteenth Century Revival",
    Edinburgh Essays on Scots Literature. Edinburgh:
    Oliver, Boyd, 1933, 73-104.

Pidal, Ramon Menéndez. Poesía Popular y Poesía
    Tradicional en la Literatura Española. Oxford:
    Imprenta Clarendonia, 1922, 36 pp.

Segar, M.C. Letter to Times Literary Supplement.
    London: (Dec. 13, 1923).

-----------. "Collection of Old Ballads", Times Literary
    Supplement. London: (Mar. 3, 1932).

Spiers, John. "The Scottish Ballads", Scrutiny, IV
    (June 1935), 35-44.

Taylor, Archer. "The Themes Common to English and
    German Balladry", Modern Language Quarterly.
    I (1940), 23-35.

t in-Je os, . " ishop . re/ . t. io o .
s ys nd tudies t f lich
coolation. I.I (19..), II0-1..

PART III

INTRODUCTORY NOTE

In the following bibliography ballad titles are
arranged in alphabetical order, and in the manner
adopted by Child all known variations of a title have
been included, and cross reference made to the best-
known title of the ballad, under which the appropriate
entry will be found.   The number given by Child is in
brackets after each ballad so numbered in The English and
Scottish Popular Ballads.   Printings of any ballad which
has a Scottish variant, or portion of one, have been given.

For simplification, and a measure of conformity,
collections, chapbooks, broadsides and periodicals have
not been separated;   chronological order only has been
adhered to.   Where publications were undated, but the
printer's name and place of publication were given, attempts
were made to ascertain when he was issuing his work, and
an approximate date was arrived at.   For brevity, works referred
to in more than one edition are distinguished by the numbers
1, 2, 3 &c.   The legend for each of these editions appears
on pages 201-203.   Since the date of publication appears
always in the left-hand column, this system need not be
confusing. The name of the library in which the work
is to be found is added in abbreviated form.   For these

188

abbreviations see page 204.

      The Child canon of ballads has not been strictly adhered to, and several ballads ap ear in this bibliography which are not in Child's collection. None in Child's collection have been omitted if they were printed during the eighteenth century.

IL Y'   I   .

YOUNG D I JN   Go

Y U G J   .   .   C.

    YOUNG L I   L L   G3   47

    Y U G T   C   Q1

Y   C   C3

The Charmer: A Collection of Songs. Edinburgh,
    1751.   Charmer 1

----------.   The Second Edition. Edinburgh, 1752.   Charmer 2

----------.   The Third Edition. Edinburgh, 1765.   Charmer 3

----------.   The Fourth Edition with improvements.
    Edinburgh, 1782.   Charmer 4

Dryden, John, ed. Miscellany Poems, containing
    a variety of new translations of the
    Ancient Poets, together with several
    original Poems. By the most eminent hands.
    4th ed. London, 1716.   Dryden 1

----------.   The Second Part of Miscellany Poems.
    London, 1716.   Dryden 2

----------.   The Third Part of Miscellany Poems.
    5th ed. London, 1727.   Dryden 3

Durfey, Thomas, ed. Wit and Mirth: or Pills to
    Purge Melancholy. London, 1712.   Durfey 1

----------.   ----------.   London, 1719.   Durfey 2

----------.   ----------.   4th ed. 1720.   Durfey 3

Lark, containing a Collection of above Four
    Hundred and Seventy celebrated English and
    Scotch Songs. London, 1740.   Lark 1

The Lark, containing a Collection of Four
    Hundred and Seventy four celebrated English
    and Scotch Songs. The Second Edition with
    Additions. London, 1742.   Lark 2

The Lark, being a Select Collection of the
    most celebrated and newest Songs, Scots
    and English. Edinburgh, 1765.   Lark 3.

The Lark, A Collection of An Hundred and Ten
    Choice Songs. Perth, 1775.   Lark 4.

Herd, David, ed. The ancient and modern Scots
    Songs, Heroic Ballads, &c. Now first
    collected into o e body, from the various
    Miscellanies, wherein they formerly
    lay dispersed. Edinburgh, 1769.   Herd 1.

----------. ----------. In two volumes. 2nd
    ed. Edinburgh, 1776.   Herd 2.

 Herd David, ed. Antient and Modern
    Scotish Songs, Heroic Ballads, &c.
    Edinburgh, 1791.   Herd 3.

 Percy Thomas, ed. Percy's Ancient Poetry,
    1st series, 3 vols.   Reliques 1.
    In Douce's Collection in the Bodleian
    Library. No title page or preliminary
    leaves. On spine Percy's Ancient
    Poetry, Vol. I. Douce has written in-
    side: "I purchased these volumes at
    D. Farmer's sale, where they were sold
    as supposed waste or imperfect; but they
    contain many pieces not in the published
    editions. See D. Farmer's notes in some
    of the pages.' Bod. Cat. gives "London,
    1764".

Percy, Thomas, ed. Reliques of Ancient English
    Poetry. London, 1765.   Reliques 2.

----------. ----------. The Second Edition.
    London, 1767.   Reliques 3.

----------. ----------. The Third Edition, London,
    1775.   Reliques 4.

----------. ----------. The Fourth Edition,
    London, 1794.   Reliques 5.

[Philips, Ambrose, ed.] A Collection of Old
    Ballads. London, 1723.   Old Ballads 1.

----------. ----------. London, 1725   Old Ballads 2.

————————. ————————. London, 1726. <u>Ol. F ll 2.</u>

————————. ————————. London, 1727. <u>Ol. F ll s 4.</u>

————————. ————————. London, 1738. <u>Ol l ll s 5.</u>

Ramsay, Allan. <u>The Ever Green, being a
    Collection of Scots Poe... wrote by the
    ingenious before 1600</u>. Edinburgh, 1724. <u>Ever Green 1.</u>

————————. ————————. Edinburgh, 1761. <u>ver Green 2.</u>

Ramsay, Allan. <u>The Te -Table Miscellany</u>.
    Edinburgh, 1723. <u>Te -T ble 1.</u>

————————. ————————. Edinburgh, 1724. <u>Te -T ble 2.</u>

————————. ————————. Volume the Second.
    Edinburgh, 1726. <u>Te -T ble 3.</u>

————————. ————————. Volume I. Edinburgh,
    1727. <u>Te -T le 4.</u>

————————. ————————. London, 1730. <u>Te -T le 5.</u>

————————. ————————. London, 1740. <u>Te -T le 6.</u>

————————. ————————. Edinburgh and Dumfries,
    1760. <u>Te -T ble 7.</u>

————————. ————————. Glasgow, 1768. <u>Te -T le 8.</u>

————————. ————————. Glasgow, 1782. <u>Te -T le 9.</u>

Thomson, William, ed. <u>Orpheus C ledonius,
    or, A Collection of the best Scotch
    Songs set to Musick by . Thomson</u>.
    London, 1725. <u>Orpheus C ledoni</u>

————————. ————————. The Second edition.
    London, 1733. <u>Orpheus C ledoni</u>

ABBREVIATIONS
OF
NAMES OF LIBRARIES

Bodleian Library, Oxford	Bod.
British Museum	B.M.
Glasgow University Library	G.U.L.
The Huntington Library, California	Hunt.
The Mitchell Library, Glasgow	M.L.
National Library of Scotland	N.L.S.
The Signet Library	S.L.
Sandeman Public Library, Perth	S.P.L.
University of British Columbia Library	U.B.C.
University of Toronto Library	U.of T.
Yale University Library	Yale

204

[itson, Joseph, ed.]   ien
  gs from the time of Kig
 enry the Third t o vol
ti n. Lo.Mon, 179 .

herd 3.

 elieves 5.

I. G LY, s e under   l

            DC

  pbook in Iauriston Castle
Collection, The iht t t
 ridge".   dinburgh, 1766.

  pbo k in L riston atle
 olle tion, " scription of
 loody Battle of othrell-
 ridge".   I o , 1772.

  I I   ILL . II

The ledonied,   ollection
 oe s written chiefly by ot
 ish th ors. London, 1775.

  vans, Tho s, ed. Old ll
4 vols. London, 1777-8d.

[itson, Joseph, ed.] ottish
 ong. 2 vols. London, 1794.

THE BATTLE OF HARLAW (163)[1]

1724	Ever Green 1.	S.P.L.
1748	Chapbook printed by Robert Foulis. Two old historical Scots Poems, giving an account of the Battles of Harlaw and the Reid-squair, "The Battle of Harlaw". Glasgow, 1748.	M.L.
1761	Ever Green 2.	Bod.
1776	Herd 2.	Bod.
1776	Dow, Daniel, ed. A Collection of Ancient Scots Music. Edinburgh, 1776.	N.L.S.
1785	[Ritson, Joseph, ed.] The Caledonian Muse. London, 1785. (Volume printed 1785, but not issued until 1821.)	Bod.
1790	Morison, R., ed. A Select Collection of Favourite Scotish Ballads. 4 vols. Perth, 1790.	Bod.
1791	Herd 2.	Bod.

THE BATTLE OF OTTERBURN (161)

1765	Reliques 2.	U.of T.
1767	Reliques 3.	U.of T.
1775	Reliques 4.	Bod.
1776	Herd 2.	Bod.
1790	Morison, R., ed. A Select Collection of Favourite Scotish Ballads. 4 vols. Perth, 1790.	Bod.
1791	Herd 2.	Bod.

---

[1] Hodgart in The Ballads states his belief that the earliest . . . . ry".

1792	[Ritson, Joseph, ed.] The North- umberland Garland. Newcastle, 1792.	Bod.
1793	[Ritson, Joseph, ed.] The North- umberland Garland, or Newcastle Nightingale. Newcastle, 1793. (This has note on flyleaf signed by F. Douce: "Given me by Mr. Ritson, the Editor.")	Bod.
1794	Reliques 5.	Bod.

THE BATTLE OF PHILIPHAUGH (202) see THE HAUGHS OF CROMDALE

THE BATTLE OF THE REID-SQUAIR

1724	Ever Green 1.	Bod.
1748	Chapbook printed by Robert Foulis. Two old historical Scots Poems, giving an account of the Battles of Harlaw and the Reid-squair. Glas- gow, 1748.	M.L.
1761	Ever Green 2.	Bod.
1776	Herd 2.	Bod.
1784	Caw, G., ed. The Poetical Museum. Hawick, 1784.	Bod.
1785	[Ritson, Joseph, ed.] The Caledon- ian Muse. London, 1785.	Bod.
1790	Morison, R., ed. A Select Collec- tion of Favourite Scottish Ballads. 4 vols. Perth, 1790.	Bod.
1791	Herd 3.	Bod.

THE BEGGAR-LADDIE (280)
(Child gives this title, but the ballad is better
known as THE GABERLUNZIE-MAN.)

1723	Tea-Table 1.	Yale
1724	Tea-Table 2.	Hunt.
1725	Old Ballads 2.	Bod.
1725	Orpheus Caledonius 1.	Bod.

1727	Tea-Table 4.
1727	A New Miscellany of Scots Songs. London, 1727. (Ramsay's portrait opp. title page.)
1730	The Merry Musician. 4 vols. London 1730
1730	Tea-Table 5.
1731	The Musical Miscellany. London, 1731.
1733	Orpheus Caledonius 2.
1734	The British Musical Miscellany or The Delightful Grove. London, 1734.
1738	Old Ballads 5.
1740	Tea-Table 6.
1752	Charmer 2.
1760	Tea-Table 7.
1764	A Choice Collection of Scotch and English Songs taken from Amaryllis, Phoenix, Orpheus, Charmer, Tea-Table, &c., &c., &c., Glasgow, 1764
1764	Reliques 1.
1765	Charmer 3.
1765	Lark 3.
1765	Reliques 2.
1767	Reliques 3.
1768	A Collection of One Hundred and Fifty Scots Songs. London, 1768.
1768	Tea-Table 8.
1769	Herd 1.

1775	Reliques 4.	U. of T.
1776	Herd 2.	Bod.
1782	Charmer 4.	N.L.S.
1782	Callander, John, ed. Two Ancient Scottish Poems: "The Gaberlunzie Man and Christ's Kirk on the Green". Edinburgh, 1782.	Bod.
1782	Tea-Table 9.	U. of T.
1783	The Blackbird, a new edition. Berwick, 1783.	Bod.
1787-1803	Johnson, James, ed. The Scots Musical Museum. 6 vols. Edinburgh, 1787-1803. No. 226.	Bod.
1790-92	A Selection of the most favourite Scots Songs, chiefly pastoral. London, 1790-92.	Bod.
1791	Herd 3.	Bod.
1794	Reliques 5.	Bod.
1794	[Ritson, Joseph, ed.] Scotish Song. 2 vols. London, 1794.	Bod.
1798	Campbell, Alexander. Introduction to the History of Poetry in Scotland . . . together with a conversation on Scotish Song . . . to which are subjoined Songs of the Lowlands of Scotland. Edinburgh, 1798.	B.M.

SY BELL AND MARY GRAY (201)

1720	Ramsay, Allan. Scots Songs. Edinburgh, 1720. (Ramsay's earliest poems were issued as booklets, 12mo, and this is a collection of these bound into one volume.)	Bod.
1720	Ramsay, Allan. Allan Ramsay's Works. Edinburgh, 1720.	Bod.

1721	Ramsay, Allan. Ramsay's Poems. Edinburgh, 1721.	.P.L.
1723	Tea-Table 1.	Yale
1724	Tea-Table 2.	Hunt.
1725	Old Ballads 3.	Lon.
1725	Orpheus Caledonius 1.	Bod.
1727	A New Miscellany of Scots Songs. London, 1727. (Ramsay's portrait opp. title page.)	Lon.
1727	Tea-Table 4.	N.L.S.
1729	The Music Miscellany. London, 1729.	Bod.
1730	Tea-Table 5.	Bod.
1733	Orpheus Caledonius 2.	Bod.
1738	Old Ballads 5.	Bod.
1738	The Vocal Miscellany. 3rd ed. London, 1738.	Lon.
1740	Tea-Table 6.	Bod.
1752	Charmer 2.	Lon.
1757	Bremner, R., ed. Thirty Scots Songs for a Voice and Harpsichord. The Music taken from the most genuine Sets extant; the words from Allan Ramsay. Edinburgh, 1757.	M.L.
1760c.	Oswald, James, ed. A Collection of the Best Old Scotch and English Songs. London.	N.L.S.
1760	Tea-Table 7.	Bod.
1764	A Choice Collection of Scotch and English Songs taken from Amaryllis, Phoenix, Orpheus, Charmer, Tea-Table &c. &c. London, 1764.	P.L.

1765	Charmer 2.	N.L.S
1765	Lark 2.	N.L.S
1768	A Collection of One Hundred and Fifty Scots Songs. London, 1768.	Bod.
1768	Tea-Table 8.	M.L.
~~1769~~	Herd 1.	G.U.L
1770c.	Thirty Scots Songs, Adapted for a voice and harpsichord by Robert Bremner. The Words by Allen Ramsey sic . London.	Bod.
1774-76	Pennant, Thomas. A Tour in Scotland and a Voyage to the Hebrides in 1772. London, 1774-76.	B.M.
1775	The Caledoniad. A Collection of Poems written chiefly by Scottish authors. London, 1775.	Bod.
1776	Herd 2.	Bod.
1780	The Chearfull Companion, containing a select Collection of Favourite Scots and English Songs, many of which are originals. Perth, 1780.	S.P.L
1782	Charmer 4.	Bod.
1782	Tea-Table 9.	U.of
1783	The Cheerful Companion, containing a select Collection of Favourite Scots and English Songs, Catches &c., many of which are original. Perth, 1783.	S.P.L
1787c.	Ramsay, Allan. "Thirty Scots Songs", in a Collection of Scots Songs. Edinburgh.	N.L.S
1787-1803	Johnson, James, ed. The Scots Musical Museum. 6 vols. Edinburgh, 1787-1803. No. 128.	Bod.
1787-88	A Collection of Scots Songs. Printed	N.L.S

| 1789 | Caliope, or English Harmony. London, 1789. | N.L. |

| 1790 | Morison, R., ed. A Select Collection of Favourite Scotish Ballads. 4 vols. Perth, 1790. | Bod. |

| 1790c. | Ramsay, Allan. Thirty Scots Songs, adapted for a voice and harpsichord by Robert Bremner. London. | M.L. |

| 1791 | Herd 3. | Bod. |

| 1792-1800 | A Selection of Scots Songs, Harmoniz- ed and Improved with Simple, and Adapted Graces . . . by Peter Urbani. Edinburgh, Glasgow, London, Dublin, 1792-1800. | Bod. |

| 1792 | Sime, D., ed. The Edinburgh Musical Miscellany. Edinburgh, Leith, Glasgow, Dundee, 1792. | Bod. |

| 1794 | [Ritson, Joseph, ed.] Scotish Song. 2 vols. London, 1794. Preface,lxv. | Bod. |

| 1795c. | Dale's Collection of Sixty Favour- ite Scotch Songs, taken from the original Manuscripts of the most Celebrated Scotch Authors and Composers. London. | Bod. |

BEWICK AND GRAHAM (211)

| 1720c | Broadside, Roxburghe Ballads. | B.M. |

| 1740c. | Broadside, "Song of Bewick and Graham". | B.M. |

BINNORIE, see under THE TWA SISTERS (10)

THE BLIND HARPER, see under THE LOCHMABEN HARPER (192)

BODOWN, see under THE TWA SISTERS (10)

THE BONNIE HOUSE O AIRLIE (199)

| 1790c | Stall copy. "The Bonnie House o Airlie". Entry taken from Child. |

1793   Thomson, George, ed. The Melodies
      of Scotland, &c. 6 vols. Edinburgh
      1793-1841.

BONNIE MILLDALE O BINNORIE, see under T E TWA
[ST RS (10)

BONNIE WEE CROODLIN DOO, see under LORD RANDAL

BY BARBARA ALLAN (84)

1740   Tea-Table 6.

1751   Charmer 1.

1760   Tea-Table 7.

1764c. Reliques 1.

1764   A Choice Collection of Scotch and
      English Songs taken from A ryllis,
      Phoenix, Orpheus, Charmer, Tea-
      Table, &c., &c., &c. Glasgow, 1764.

1765   Reliques 2.

1767   Reliques 3.

1768   Tea-Table 8.

1769   Herd 1.

1775   Reliques 4.

1776   Herd 2.

1782   Tea-Table 9.

1787-1803 Johnson, James, ed. The Scots
      Musical Museum. 6 vols. Edinburgh,
      1787-1803. No. 221.

1790   Morison, ., ed. A Select Collectio
      of Favourite Scottish Ballads. 4 vol
      Perth, 1790.

1790-92 A Selection of the most favourite
      Scots Songs, chiefly Pastoral.
      2 vols. London, 1790-92.

1792   The Poetical Epitome, or, Elegant
                 Extracts, abridged. London, 1792.

1794   Reliques 2.

1794   [Ritson, Joseph, ed.] Scotish Song.
                 2 vols. London, 1794.

1796   Elegant Extracts or useful and
                 entertaining Pieces of Poetry.
                 London, 1796.

1798   Campbell, Alexander. An introduction
                 to the History of Poetry in Scotland
                 ... together with a conversation on
                 Scotish Song ..., to which are sub-
                 joined Songs of the Lowlands of Scot-
                 land. Edinburgh, 1798.

NY BEE HOM (92)

1776   Herd 2.

1787-1803 Johnson, James, ed. The Scots
                 Musical Museum. 6 vols. Edinburgh,
                 1787-1803. No. 115.

1792-1800 A Selection of Scots Songs, Harmon-
                 ized and Improved with Simple and
                 Adapted Graces ... by Peter Urbani.
                 Edinburgh, Glasgow, London, Dublin.

1794   [Ritson, Joseph, ed.] Scotish Song.
                 2 vols. London, 1794.

BONNY EARL OF LIVINGSTON, see under FAIR MARY
F WALLINGTON (91)

BONNY EARL OF MURRAY (181)

1733   Orpheus Caledonius 2.

1740   Tea-Table 6.

1760   Tea-Table 7.

1764   A choice Collection of Scotch and
                 English Songs taken from Argyllis,
                 Phoenix, Orpheus, Charmer, Tea-
                 Table &c. &c. &c. Glasgow, 1764.

1764c.	Reliques 1.	Bod.
1765	Reliques 2.	U.of T.
1767	Reliques 3.	U.of T.
1768	Tea-Table 8.	M.L.
1769	Herd 1.	G.U.L.
1775	Reliques 4.	U.of T.
1776	Herd 2.	Bod.
1781	Pinkerton, John, ed. Scotish Tragic Ballads. London, 1781.	Bod.
1782	Tea-Table 9.	U.of T.
1783	Pinkerton, John, ed. Select Scotish Ballads. London, 1783.	B.M.
1787-1803	Johnson, James, ed. The Scots Musical Museum. 6 vols. Edinburgh, 1787-1803. No. 177.	Bod.
1787-88	A Collection of Scots Songs. Printed by Neil Stewart. Edinburgh.	N.L.S.
1790	Morison, R., ed. A select Collection of Favourite Scotish Ballads. 4 vols. Perth, 1790.	Bod.
1790-92	A Selection of the most favourite Scots Songs, chiefly pastoral. 2 vols. London, 1790-92.	Bod.
1791	Herd 3.	Bod.
1794	Reliques 5.	Bod.
1794	[Ritson, Joseph, ed.] Scotish Song. 2 vols. London, 1794.	Bod.

BONNY LASS OF LOCHROYAN, see under THE LASS F ROCH ROYAN (76)

NY LIZIE BAILLIE (227)

1776	Herd 2.	Bod.

1787-1803	Johnson, James, e.. The Scots Music l Museum. 6 vols. Edinburgh, 1787-1803. No. 456.	Bod.
1790-92	A Selection of the most favourite Scots songs, chiefly pastoral. 2 vols. London, 1790-92.	Bod.
1791	Herd 3.	o..
1795	Chapbook in Kidment's Collection. Popular Poetry, "Bonny Lizie Baillie" 1795.	C.U.L.
1796c.	Chapbook, A Right Merrie Book of Garlands and Songs, "Bonny Lizie Baillie". Aberdeen.	Bod.
1750-1812	Chapbook in Motherwell's Collection, part of Lauriston Castle Collection.	N.L.S.
1750-1800	Chapbook, J. and M. Robertson. Glasgow.	N.L.S.

BONNY MAY, see under THE BROOM OF COWDENKNOWS (217)

BOTHWELL, see under GIL MORTON (5)

BOTHWELL BRIDGE (206), see under THE BATTLE OF BOTHWELL BRIDGE

THE BRAES OF YARROW (214)

1730	Tea-Table 5.	Bod.
1733	Orpheus Caledonius 2.	Bod.
1740	Tea-Table 6.	Bod.
1751	Charmer 1.	Bod.
1757	Bremner, R., ed. Thirty Scots Songs for Voice and Harpsichord. The Music taken from the most genuine Sets extant; the Words from Allan Ramsay. Edinburgh, 1757.	B.L.
1760	Tea-Table 7.	Bod.
1764	A choice Collection of Scotch and English Songs, taken from Amaryllis, Phoenix, Orpheus, Charmer, Tea-Table ... 1764.	S.B.L.

1764c.	Reliques 1.	Po...
1765	Reliques 2.	U.c
1765	Lark 3.	N.I
1767	Reliques 3.	U.c
1768	A Collection of One Hundred and Fifty Scots Songs. London, 1768.	Po...
1768	Tea-Table 8.	N.I
1775	The Caledoniad. A Collection of Poems, written chiefly by Scottish authors. London, 1775.	Lo...
1775	Lark 4.	N.I
1775	Reliques 4.	U.c
1782	Chapter 4.	N.I
1782	Tea-Table 9.	U.c
1784	Chapbook in Maidment's Collection. Popular Poetry, "The Dairy Maid or Vocal miscellany". Edinburgh, 1784.	C.L
1790	Morison, R., ed. A Select Collection of Favourite Scottish Ballads. 4 vols. Perth, 1790.	Bod
1790-92	A Selection of the most favourite Scots Songs, chiefly pastoral. 2 vols. London, 1790-92.	Po...
1790c.	Ramsay, Allan. Thirty Scots Songs, adapted for a voice and harpsichord by Robert Bremner. London.	N.I
1790c.	Bremner, R. The Second Set of Scots Songs adapted for a voice and harpsichord by Robert Bremner. Edinburgh.	N.I
1791	Herd 2.	Bod
1792	The Poetic Epitome, or Elegant ... ... London, 1792.	L...

1794	Reliques 5.	Bod.
1794	[Ritson, Joseph, ed.] Scotish Song. 2 vols. London, 1794. (There are two variants here.)	Bod.
1796	Elegant Extracts; or useful and entertaining Pieces of Poetry. London, 1796.	B.M.

BROOM BLOOMS BONNIE, see under THE BREATH
ND KNIFE (16)

BROOM OF COWDENKNOWS (217)

1738	Old Ballads 5.	Bod.
1769	Herd 1.	G.U.L
1775	The Caledoniad. A Collection of Poems, written chiefly by Scottish authors. London, 1775.	Bod.
1776	Herd 2.	Bod.
1787-1803	Johnson, James, ed. The Scots Musical Museum. 6 vols. Edinburgh, 1787-1803. No. 110.	Bod.
1791	Herd 3.	Bod.
1750-1812	Chapbook in Motherwell's Collection, part of Laurieston Castle Collection, no date, or place of publication.	N.L.S

BROOKFIELD HILL (43)

1769	Herd 1.	G.U.L
1776	Herd 2.	Bod.
1791	Herd 3.	Bod.

1755	Chapbook printed by Robert and Andrew Foulis, "Adam of Gordon", an ncient Scottish Poem. Glasgow, 1775.	M.L
1765	Reliques 2.	U.o
1767	Reliques 3.	U.o
1768	A Collection of One Hundred and Fifty Scots Songs. London, 1768.	Bod
1769	Herd 1.	G.U
1775	Reliques 4.	U.o
1776	Herd 2.	Bod
1781	Pinkerton, John, ed. Scotish Tragic Ballads. London, 1781.	Bod
1783	Pinkerton, John, ed. Select Scotish Ballads. London, 1783.	F.W
1790	Morison, R., ed. A Select Collection of Favourite Scotish Ballads. 4 vols. Perth, 1790.	Bod
1790	[Ritson, Joseph, ed.] Ancient Songs from the time of King Henry the Third to the Revolution. London, 1790.	Bod
1791	Herd 3.	Bod
1794	Reliques 5.	Bod
1794	[Ritson, Joseph, ed.] Scotish Songs. 2 vols. London, 1794.	Bod
1796c.	Chapbook, A Right Merrie Book of Garlands and Songs, "Two Excellent New Songs". Aberdeen.	Bod

GLEN DEARMONT'S COURTSHIP (46)

1735   The New British Songster. Falkirk,
1735.
    (Child gives this entry.)

1750-1800   Chapbook, J. and M. Robertson.
Glasgow.   N.L.S

GY CHASE, see under THE HUNTING OF THE CHEVIOT (162)

GIL MAURICE (83)

1755   Chapbook printed by Robert and
Andrew Foulis. Gill Morice, an
ancient Scottish Poem. 2nd ed.
Glasgow, 1755.   M.L.

1757   Bremner, R., ed. Thirty Scots
Songs for a Voice and Harpsichord.
The Music taken from the most
genuine Sets extant; the words from
Allan Ramsay. Edinburgh, 1757.   M.L.

1765   Lark 3.   N.L.S

1764   Reliques 1.   Lou.

1765   Reliques 2.   U.of

1767   Reliques 3.   U.of

1768   A Collection of One Hundred and
Fifty Scots Songs. London, 1768.   Bod.

1769   Herd 1.   C.U.L

1775   The Caledoniad. A Collection of
Poems, written chiefly by Scottish
authors. London, 1775.   Bod.

1775   Reliques 4.   U.of

1776   Herd 2.   Bod.

1781   Pinkerton, John, ed. Scottish
Tragic Ballads. London, 1781.   Bod.

1783   Pinkerton, John, ed. Select
            Scottish ballads. London, 1783.   B.M

1784   Caw, G., ed. The Poetical Museum.
            Hawick, 1784.   Bo

1785c.   Chapbook in Lauriston Castle Collec-
            tion, "Gill Morice". Edinburgh.   N.L

1787-1803   Johnson, James, ed. The Scots
            Musical Museum. 6 vols. Edinburgh,
            1787-1803. No. 203.   Bod

1790   Morison, R., ed. A Select Collec-
            tion of Favourite Scottish ballads.
            4 vols. Perth, 1790.   Bod

1890-92   A Collection of the most favourite
            Scots Songs, chiefly pastoral.
            2 vols. London, 1790-92.   Bod

1790c.   Ramsay, Allan. Thirty Scots Songs,
            printed for a voice and harpsichord
            by Robert Bremner. London.   N.L

1791   Herd 2.   Bod

1794   Reliques 2.   Bo

1794   [Ritson, Joseph, ed.] Scottish Song.
            2 vols. London, 1794.   Bo

1795c.   Chapbook in Maidment's Collection.
            Popular Poetry.   C.L

1795c.   Dale's Collection of Sixty favourite
            Scotch Songs, taken from the original
            Manuscripts of the most Celebrated
            Scotch Authors and Composers.
            London.   Bod

1795   Chapbook printed by Cameron and
            Murdoch. Poetry, Original and
            Selected. Glasgow, 1795.   N.L

1796   Chapbook in Maidment's Collection.
            Popular Poetry.   C.L

1796	Chapbooks, Scotish Ballads and Songs. Manchester, 1796.	Bod.
1798	Campbell, Alexander. An Introduction to the History of Poetry in Scotland ... together with a conversation on Scotish Songs ... to which are subjoined songs of the Lowlands of Scotland. Edinburgh, 1798.	E.M.
1799c.	Chapbook, J. and M. Robertson. Glasgow.	M.L.
1799	Chapbook, Garland of Ballads. Paisley, 1799.	C.U.L.

CHILD OF ELLE, see under EARL BRAND (7)

CHILD WATERS (63)

1764c.	Pelican 1.	Bod.
1765	Pelican 2.	U.of T.
1767	Pelican 3.	U.of T.
1769	Herd 1.	G.U.L.
1775	Pelican 4.	U.of T.
1777-84	Evans, Thomas, ed. Old Ballads. 4 vols. London, 1777-84.	Bod.
1790	Morison, R., ed. A Select Collection of Favourite Scotish Ballads. 4 vols. Perth, 1790.	Bod.
1792	The Poetic Epitome; or Elegant Extracts abridged. London, 1792.	Bod.
1794	Pelican 5.	Bod.

EARL COLVILL (42)

1769	Herd 1.	G.U.L.
1776	Herd 2.	Bod.

| 1790 | Morison, R., ed. _A Select Collection of Favourite Scotish Ballads_. 4 vols. Perth, 1790. | Bod. |
| 1791 | _Herd 3_. | Bod. |

THE COMPLAINT OF SCOTLAND, see under THE HUNTING OF THE CHEVIOT (162)

THE CROODLIN DOO, see under LORD RANDAL (12)

CRUEL BROTHER (11)

1776	_Herd 2_.	Bod.
1787-1803	Johnson, James, ed. _The Scots Musical Museum_. 6 vols. Edinburgh, 1787-1803. No. 320.	Bod.
1790	Morison, R., ed. _A Select Collection of Favourite Scotish Ballads_. 4 vols. Perth, 1790.	Bod.
1791	_Herd 3_.	Bod.

THE CRUEL KNIGHT, see under YOUNG JOHNSONE (88)

THE CRUEL SISTER, see under THE TWA SISTERS (10)

CRUEL WILLIAM, see under CHILD WATERS (63)

THE DEATH OF QUEEN JANE (170)

| 1723 | _Old Ballads 1_. | U.B.C. |
| 1777-84 | Evans, Thomas, ed. _Old Ballads_. 4 vols. London, 1777-84. | Bod. |

DICK O THE COW (185)

| 1774-76 | Pennant, Thomas, _Pennant's Tour in Scotland and Voyage to the Hebrides in 1772_. London, 1774-76. | B.M. |
| 1784 | Caw, G., ed. _The Poetical Museum_. Hawick, 1784. | Bod. |

THE DOUGLAS TRAGEDY, see under EARL BRAND (7)

E OF GORDON'S D.UGHTER (237)

1785	Chapbook in Lauriston Castle Collection, "Duke of Gordon's Three Daughters". Edinburgh, 1785.	N.L.S.
1785	Chapbook in Lauriston Castle Collection, "The Duke of Gordon's Daughters and Capt in Ogilvy". Stirling, 1785.	N.L.S.
1785	Chapbook, "The Duke of Gordon's Three Daughters". Dumfries, 1785.	B.M.
1787-1803	Johnson, James, ed. The Scots Musical Museum. 6 vols. Edinburgh, 1787-1803. No. 419.	Bod.
1794	[Ritson, Joseph, ed.] Scotish Songs. 2 vols. London, 1794.	Bod.
1795	Chapbook in Madment's Collection, Popular Poetry, "Miscellaneous Ballads", "Duke of Gordon's Daughters". 1795.	G.U.L.
1796	Chapbook in Madment's Collection, Popular Poetry, "Duke of Gordon's Three Daughters", 1796.	G.U.L.

L ERAND (7)

1765	Reliques 2.	U. of T.
1767	Reliques 3.	U. of T.
1775	Reliques 4.	U. of T.

1783	Pinkerton, John, ed. Select Scotish Ballads. London, 1783.	L. .
1784	Caw, G., ed. The Poetical Museum. Hawick, 1784.	Bod.
1790	Morison, R., ed. Select Collection of Favourite Scotish Ballads. 4 vols. Perth, 1790.	Bod.
1791	Herd 3.	Bod.
1794	Reliques 5.	Bod.
1796	Chapbooks, Scottish Ballads and Songs. Manchester, 1796.	Bod.
1750-1812	Chapbook in Motherwell's Collection, part of Lauriston Castle Collection, "The Douglas Tragedy".	N.L.S.

EARL RICHARD, see under THE KNIGHT AND THE SHEPHERD'S DAUGHTER (110)
EDOM O GORDON, see under CAPTAIN CAR (178)
EDWARD, EDWARD (13)

1765	Reliques 2.	U. of T.
1767	Reliques 2.	U. of T.
1768	A Collection of One Hundred and Fifty Scots Songs. London, 1768.	Bod.
1775	Reliques 4.	U. of T.
1776	Herd 2.	Bod.
1781	Pinkerton, John, ed. Scotish Tragic Ballads. London, 1781.	Bod.
1783	Pinkerton, John, ed. Select Scotish Ballads. London, 1783.	C.M.
1790	Morison, R., ed. Select Collection of Favourite Scotish Ballads. 4 vols. Perth, 1790.	Bod.
1791	Herd 3.	Bod.

94   [Ritson, Joseph, ed.] Scotish
2 vols. London, 1794.

ANNIE (62)

69   Herd 1.

76   Herd 2.

91   Herd 3.

94   [Ritson, Joseph, ed.] Scotish
2 vols. London, 1794.

IP ANNIE AND S ... ILLI , see under LO
. ..KI AI .T (73)

HELEN

74-76   Pennant, Thomas. A Tour in Sc
and a Voyage to the Hebrides 1
London, 1774-76.

74   Dumfries eekly Magazine, 7 Ju
1774. Dumfries.

76   [Tait, John, ed.] Scots Poetic
Legends. London, 1776.

81   Pinkerton, John, ed. Scotish
Tragic Ballads. London, 1781.

83   Pinkerton, John, ed. Select S
ish Ballads. London, 1783.

87-1803 Johnson, James, ed. The Scots
usical useum. 6 vols. Edin
1787-1803. A.O. 155.

90-92   A Selection of the most favour
Scots Songs, chiefly pastoral.
2 vols. London. 1790-92.

1791	Laurie's Scottish Songs, I.	
	(Entry taken from Child.)	
1791	Herd 2.	Do.
1794	[Ritson, Joseph, ed.] Scotish Songs. 2 vols. London, 1794.	Do.
1794	Sinclair's Statistical Account of Scotland XIII.	
	(Entry taken from Child.)	

FAIR ISABELL OF ROCHROYALL, see under THE LASS OF ROCH ROYAN (76)

FAIR JANET (64)

1769	Herd 1.	G.U.L.
1776	Herd 2.	Do.
1794	[Ritson, Joseph, ed.] Scotish Songs. 2 vols. London, 1794.	Bod.

FAIR MABEL OF WALLINGTON, see under FAIR MARY OF WALLINGTON (91)

FAIR MARGARET, see under CHILD WATERS (63)

FAIR MARGARET AND SWEET WILLIAM (74)

1711	"William and Margret", an Old Ballad.	
	(Intry taken from Child.)	
1725	Orpheus Caledonius 1.	Bod.
1726	Tea-Table 3.	N.L.S.
1727	A New Miscellany of Scotish Songs. London, 1727.	
	(Ramsay's portrait on title page.)	Bod.
1730	Tea-Table 5.	Do.
1733	Orpheus Caledonius 2.	Do.
1738	Old Ballads 5.	Do.
1738	The Vocal Miscellany. 3rd. ed. London, 1738.	Bod.

1740	Tea-Table 6.	Bod.
1752	Charmer 2.	Bod.
1760	Tea-Table 7.	Bod.
1764	A Choice Collection of Scotch and English Songs, taken from Ambrville, Phoenix, Orpheus, Charmer, Tea-Table, &c., &c., &c. Glasgow, 1764.	E.P.
1764c.	Reliques 1.	Bod.
1765	Charmer 3.	N.L.
1765	Reliques 2.	U.of
1767	Reliques 3.	U.of
1768	A Collection of One Hundred and Fifty Scots Songs. London, 1768.	Lo.
1768	Tea-Table 8.	N.L.
1769	Herd 1, "Fair Margaret and Sweet William" and "William and Margaret".	G.U.
1775	Lark 4.	N.L.
1775	Reliques 4.	U.of
1776	Herd 2, "Fair Margaret and Sweet William" and "William and Margaret".	Bod.
1782	Charmer 4.	N.L.
1782	Tea-Table 9.	U.of
1783	The Blackbird, a new edition. Lerwick, 1783.	Bod.
1790	Morison, R., ed. A Select Collection of Favourite Scottish Ballads. 2 vols. Perth, 1790.	Bod.
1790-92	A Selection of the most favourite Scots Songs, chiefly pastoral. London, 1790-92.	Lo.

1791   herd ?. "Fair Margaret and Sweet
            William", and "William and Margaret"

1794   Reliques 5.

1794   [Ritson, Joseph, ed.]   Scotish Song.
            2 vols. London, 1794.

1798   Chapbooks printed by Brash and Reid.
            Poetry: original and selected, 1798

1750-1812   Chapbooks in Lauriston Castle Collec-
            tion. "The Woeful Tragedy of
            William and Margaret", Stirling, and
            "The Tragical End of William and
            Margaret", Stirling, and "William
            and Margaret's Ghost", Edinburgh.

1750-1812   Chapbooks in Motherwell's Collec-
            tion, Part of Lauriston Castle
            Collection, Leeds.

1799c.   Chapbook, J. and M. Robertson, "The
            Tragical End of William and Margaret
            Glasgow.

FAIR MARGARET'S MISFORTUNE, see under FAIR MARGARET
AND SWEET WILLIAM (74)

FAIR MARY OF WALLINGTON (91)

1793   [Ritson, Joseph, ed.] The North-
            umberland Garland: or Newcastle
            Nightingale, "Fair Mabel of Walling-
            ton". Newcastle, 1793.

FAIR FLOWER KNIGHT OUTWITTED, see under LADY ISABEL AND
THE ELF-KNIGHT (4)

FAMOUS FLOWER OF SERVING-MEN (106)

1723   Old Ballads 1.

1765   Reliques 2.

1767   Reliques 3.

1775   Reliques 4.

1783   [Ritson, Joseph, ed.] A Select
              Collection of English Songs... ith
              their origin 1 irs. 3 vols.
              London, 1783.

1794   Reliques 5.

FALSE SIR JOHN, see under LADY ISABEL AND THE ELF-
   KNIGHT (4)

FINE FLOWERS IN THE VALLEY, see under THE CRUEL BROTHER

THE FIRE OF FRENDRAUGHT (196)

1776   Herd 2.

1787-1803 Johnson, James, ed. The Scots
              Musical Museum. 6 vols. Edinburgh,
              1787-1803. No. 286.

1790   Morison, R., ed. A Select Collection
              of Favourite Scotish Ballads. 4 vols.
              Perth, 1790.

1791   Herd 3.

1794   [Ritson, Joseph, ed.] Scotish Songs.
              2 vols. London, 1794.

FLODDEN FIELD (168)

1790   [Ritson, Joseph, ed.] Ancient Songs
              from the time of King Henry the Third
              to the Revolution. London, 1790.

GABERLUNZIE MAN, see under THE BEGGAR-LADDIE (280)

THE GALLANT GRAHAMS OF SCOTLAND

1768   A Collection of One Hundred and
              Fifty Scots Songs. London, 1768.

XIT (209)

.784   [Ritson, Joseph, ed.] The Northern
Garland, "Come you lusty northerne
lads". Stockton, 1784.

1787-1803 Johnson, James, ed. The Scots
Musical Museum. 6 vols. 1787-1803.
No. 346.

UP AND BAR THE DOOR (275)

.769   Herd 1.

.776   Herd 2.

.777   Chapbook, Edinburgh, 1777.

.782   Charmer 4.

1787-1803 Johnson, James, ed. The Scots
Musical Museum. 6 vols. Edinburgh,
1787-1803. No. 300.

1790   Morison, R., ed. A Select Collection of Favourite Scottish Ballads.
4 vols. Perth, 1790.

1791   Herd 3.

1794   [Ritson, Joseph, ed.] Scotish Songs.
2 vols. London, 1794.

1796c.   Chapbook in Malament's Collection,
Popular Poetry, "Get up and Bar the
Door". Dunbar.

1798   Campbell, Alexander. An Introduction
to the History of Poetry in Scotland
. . . together with a conversation on
Scotish Song . . . to which are sub-
joined . . . of the Lowlands of Scotland. Edinburgh, 1798.

OLD LADY, see under XURLIN (209)

URPENTON (5)

1769   Herd 1.

1775	Herd 1.	Bo'.
1790	Morison, R., ed. Select Collection of Favourite Scotish Ballads. 4 vols. Perth, 1790.	Bod.
1791	Herd 2.	Bod.

NO ICE, see under CHILD MAURICE (83)

DEROY

1716	Dryden 1.	Bod.
1719	Durfey 2.	Bo..
1723	Old Ballads 1.	U.L.(
1727	Dryden 3.	Bod.
1727	Old Ballads 4.	Bod.
1733	Orpheus Caledonius 2.	Bo..
1740	L.M 1.	N.L..
1765	Reliques 2.	U.of
1767	Reliques 3.	U.of
1768	A Collection of One Hundred and Fifty Scots Songs. London, 1768.	Bo..
1769	Herd 1.	G.U.L
1775	Reliques 4.	U.of
1776	Herd 2.	Bod.
1790	Morison, R., ed. A Select Collection of Favourite Scotish Ballads. 4 vols. Perth, 1790.	Bo..
1791	Herd 3.	Bo..
1792	The Poetical Epitome, or Elegant Extracts Abridged. London, 1792.	Bo.
1794	Reliques 5.	Bod.

1794	[Ritson, Joseph, ed.] _Scotish Song._ 2 vols. London, 1794.
1796	_Elegant Extracts, or useful and entertaining Pieces of Poetry._ London, 1796
1796	_Chapbook, Scotish Ballads and Songs._ Manchester, 1796.
1798	Campbell, Alexander. _An Introduction to the History of Poetry in Scotland . . . together with a conversation on Scotish Song . . . to which are subjoined Songs of the Lowlands of Scotland._ Edinburgh, 1798.
1750-1800	Chapbook, J. and M. Robertson in the Saltmarket, Glasgow.

GLASGERION (67)

1764c.	_Reliques 1._
1765	_Reliques 2._
1767	_Reliques 3._
1775	_Reliques 4._
1794	_Reliques 5._

KINLIE, see under GLASGERION (67)

GOODMAN OF AUCHTERMOUCHTIE, see under THE WIFE OF AUCHTERMOUCHTY

GOWANS SAE GAY, see under LADY ISABEL AND THE ELF KNIGHT (4)

GREY COCK; O., SAY YOU MY FATHER? (248)

1769	_Herd 1._
1772	_Vocal Music, or the Songster's Companion._ London, 1772. (Entry taken from Child.)

1776	Herd 2.	Eo
1783	Pinkerton, John, ed. Select Scotish Ballads. London, 1783.	Lo
1787-1803	Johnson, James, ed. The Scots Musical Museum. 5 vols. Edinburgh, 1787-1803. No. 76.	Eod
1795c.	Dale's Collection of sixty Favourite Scotch Songs. London.	Lo

GYPSI COME TO OUR GOOD LORD'S GATE, see under
THE GYPSY LADDIE (200)

GYPSY LADDIE (200)

1740	Tea-Table 6.	Eo
1751	Charmer 1.	Eo
1760	Tea-Table 7.	Lo
1768	A Collection of One Hundred and Fifty Scots Songs. London, 1768.	Lo
1768	Tea-Table 8.	M.L
1769	Herd 1.	G.U
1775	Collection of Chapbooks, The Songster's Magazine, "The Rural Lovers Delight" contains "The Gypsey Laddy". London, 1775.	B.M
1776	Herd 2.	Lo
1782	Tea-Table 9.	U.o
1787-1803	Johnson, James, ed. The Scots Musical Museum. 6 vols. Edinburgh, 1787-1803. No. 181.	Eod
1787-88	A Collection of Scots Songs. Edinburgh.	M.L
1790	Morison, R., ed. A Select Collection of Favourite Scotish Ballads. 4 vols. Perth, 1790.	Lod

1790	A Selection of the most favourite Scots Songs, chiefly pastoral. London, 1790.	Lo:
1791	Herd 3.	Ho
1794	[Ritson, Joseph, ed.] Scotish Song. 2 vols. London, 1794.	Lo:

YKNUTE

1719	Anonymous Pamphlet, printed in Edinburgh, 1719.	Po:
1724	Ever Green 1.	Lo:
1730	Tea-Table 5.	Ho:
1740	Tea-Table 6.	Ho
1745	Chapbook printed by Robert Foulis. [Wardlaw, Lady Elizabeth.] "Hardyknute, a fragment of an antient Scots poem". Glasgow, 1745.	M.I
1748	Chapbook printed by Robert Foulis. [Wardlaw, Lady Elizabeth.] "Hardyknute, a fragment of an antient Scots poem". Glasgow, 1748.	M.I
1753	Warton, Thomas. The Union; or select Scots and English Poems. Edinburgh, 1853.	G.C
1754	Chapbook. Scottish Poetry, "Hardyknute". Aberdeen, 1754.	M.I
1760	Tea-Table 7.	Lo:
1761	Ever Green 2.	Lo:
1764	A Choice Collection of Scotch and English Songs taken from Myrtillis, Phoenix, Orpheus, Charmer, Tea-Table, &c., &c., &c. Glasgow, 1764.	.F
1764c.	Reliques 1.	Ho:
1765	Reliques 2.	U.c

1767	Reliques 3.
176.	A Collection of One Hundred and Fifty Scots Songs. London, 1768.
1768	Tea-Table 8.
1769	Herd 1.
1775	The Caledoniad, A Collection of Poems, written chiefly by Scottish Authors. London, 1775.
1775	Reliques 4.
1776	Herd 2.
1781	Pinkerton, John, ed. Scotish Tragic Ballads. London, 1781.
1782	Tea-Table 9.
1784	Caw, G., ed. The Poetical Museum. Hawick, 1784.
1787-1803	Johnson, James, ed. The Scots Musical Museum. 6 vols. Edinburgh, 1787-1803. No. 280.
1790	Morison, R., ed. A Select Collection of favourite Scotish Ballads. 4 vols. Perth, 1790.
1790-1792	A Selection of the ost favourite Scots Songs, chiefly pastoral. 2 vols. London, 1790-92.
1791	Herd 3.
1794	Reliques 5.
1794	[Ritson, Joseph, ed.] Scotish Song. 2 vols. London, 1794.

THE HAUGHS OF CROMDALE

| 1776 | Chapbooks. "The Haughs of Cromdale". Banff, Aberdeen, Elgin, 1776. |

1787-1803   Johnson, Jame , ed. The cots
            uic l Museum. 6 vols. dinburgh,
            1787-1803. No. 4 8.

1794   [Ritson, Jo eph, ed.] coti h on .
            2 vols. London, 1794.

1795   Chapbook in M ilment's Coll ction,
            Po ul r Poetry, "The H ughs of Crom-
            d le". 1795.

1798   C mpbell, Alexa der. n Introduc-
            tion to the Hi tory f oetry in
            cotl nd . . . . to ether ith
            conver tion on cotish ong . . .
            to hich re ubjoined ome of the
            Lo i nt of cotl nd. dinburgh,
            1798.

1799   Chapbook, J. nd . Robertson, "The
            H ughs of Crumbel".. Gl sgow, 1799.

1750-1812   Chapbook in Motherwell's Collection,
            p rt of L uriston C stle Collection,
            "A Memor ble B ttle fought by the
            gre t Montro e g inst Oliver Crom-
            wel (sic) upon the H ughs of Crumdel"

1799c.   Chapbook in Motherwell' Collection,
            p rt of L uriston C stle Collection,
            " Memor ble B ttle fou ht by the
            gre t Montro e g inst Oliver Crom-
            wel upon the H ughs of Crumbel".

HAWS OF C UMDEL, see under THE H UGHS OF C O D L

P I OF LIN, see under T L IE OF LI E (267)

H I OF LINE (267)

1765   eliques 2.

1767   eliques 2.

1769   Herd 1.

1775   Reliques 4.

4   Cay, G., ed. The Poetical Museum.
         Hawick, 1784.

5   Chapbook in Lauriston Castle Collec-
         tion, "The Heir of Linne". Edin-
         burgh, 1785.

4   Reliques 5.

4   [Ritson, Joseph, ed.] Scottish Songs.
         2 vols. London, 1794.

R OF LYNNE, see under THE HEIR OF LINNE (161

P KIRKCONNELL, see under FAIR HELEN

ELM (189)

4   Cay, G., ed. The Poetical Museum.
         Hawick, 1784.

LINCOLN, see under THE JEW'S DAUGHTER (155)

ELME (191)

9   Durfey 2.

7-1803   Johnson, James, ed. The Scots
         Musical Museum. 6 vols. Edinburgh,
         1787-1803. No. 303.

0   [Ritson, Joseph, ed.] Ancient
         Songs from the time of King Henry
         the Third to the revolution.
         London, 1790.

0-1800   Chapbooks, J. and M. Robertson in
         the Saltmarket. Glasgow.

S OF CHEVIT, see under THE HUNTING OF THE
OT (162)

TING OF THE CHEVIOT (162)

9   Durfey 2.

3   Old Ballads 1.

7   Dryden 3.

1727	Old Ballads 2.	Bod.
1747	Chapbook printed by Robert Foulis, "Chevy Chase", according to all the Scottish editions. Glasgow, 1747.	M.L.
1752	Charmer 2.	Bod.
1754	Chapbooks, Scottish Poetry, "Chevy Chase . . .". Aberdeen, 1754.	M.L.
1757	Bremner, R., ed. Thirty Scots Songs for a Voice and Harpsichord. The music taken from the most genuine sets extant: the words from Allan Ramsay. Edinburgh, 1757.	M.L.
1764 c.	Reliques 1. "The Ancient Ballad of Chevy Chase", and "The more modern Ballad of Chevy Chase".	Bod.
1765	The Annual Register, or a View of the History, Politics and Literature for the Year 1765. London. (Republished by Dodsley, 1793.)	Bod.
1765	Charmer 2.	N.L.S
1765	Reliques 2, as in Reliques 1.	U.of
1767	Reliques 3, as in Reliques 1.	U.of
1775	The Caledoniad. A Collection of Poems written chiefly by Scottish Authors. London, 1775.	Bod.
1775	Reliques 4, as in Reliques 1.	U.of
1776	Herd 2.	Bod.
1777	Chapbook, "The Hunting of Chievy Chase". Edinburgh, 1777.	C.U.L
1782	Charmer 4.	N.L.S
1783	The Blackbird, a new edition. Berwick, 1783.	Bod.

1783	A Select Collection of English Songs. 2 vols. London, 1733.	B.M.
1785	Chapbook in Lauriston Castle Collection, "An excellent old ballad describing the Woeful Hunting and famous battle on Chevy Chace". Stirling, 1785.	N.L.S.
1735c.	Chapbook in Lauriston Castle Collection, "The Hunting of Chevy Chace". Edinburgh.	N.L.S.
1790	Morison, R., ed. A Select Collection of Favourite Scotish Ballads. 4 vols. Perth, 1790.	Bod.
1790	Ramsay, Allan. Thirty Scots Songs, adapted for a voice and harpsichord by Robert Bremner. London, 1790.	M.L.
1791	Herd 3.	Bod.
1792	The Poetical Epitome, or Elegant Extracts, abridged. London, 1792.	B.M.
1793	The Northumberland Garland; or Newcastle Nightingale, "The Hunting of the Cheviat" and "The Hunting in Chevy Chase". Newcastle, 1793.	Bod.
1794	Reliques 5, as in Reliques 1.	Bod.
1795c.	Dale's Collection of sixty favourite Scotch Songs, taken from the original Manuscripts of the most Celebrated Scotch Authors and Composers. London.	Bod.
1797	Chapbooks, Scottish Ballads and Songs. Manchester, 1797.	Bod.
1798	Chapbook, Brash and Reid, Poetry; original and selected. Glasgow, 1798.	B.M.
1799c.	Chapbook, Garland of Ballads. Paisley.	G.U.L.

1712-1822 Ch____, "History of t__ ___tle
           on Chevy-Ch__ce". Stirling, _ in-
           burgh, F_lkirk, Lon_on, 1712-1822.   G.J.L.

IN AUCHTERMUCHTY B_ILT A M_N, see under T___ _R_ OF
_UGHT_RMUCHTY

I'LL _O LY B__ST _____A', see under C_PT_IN _____D'N'
COURTSHIP (46)

I'LL _AGER, I'LL _AG_R, see under BROOMFI_LD HILL (43)

I'_I._I ___ __-___ _ N LI__, see under _ _IR_ _AN
JAMIE DOUGLAS (204) see under WALE' WALE' UP YON BANK
THE J__' _L_GONTR_ (155)

1765	Reliques 2.	U. of T.
1767	Reliques 2.	U. of T.
176_	Herd 1.	G.U.L.
1775	Reliques 4.	U. of T.
1776	Herd 2.	Iod.
1781	_inkerton, John, ed. Scotish Tragic B_lla_s. Lon_on, 1781.	Bo_.
1783	Pinkerton, John, ed. Select Scotish Balla_s. Lon_on, 1783.	Io_.
1787-1803	Johnson, J_mes, ed. The _cots Music_l _useum. 6 vols. Edinburgh, 1787-180_. No. 58_.	Bo_.
1790	Morison, R., ed. _ Select Collec-tion of _ vourite Scotish B_lla_s. 4 vols. Perth, 1790.	bo_.
1791	Herd 3.	Io_.
1794	Reliques 5.	Bo_.

JOCK O THE _I_E (187)

1794	C_w, _., ed. The Poetic_l Museum. H_wick, 1784.	Io_.

JOHNIE ARMSTRONG (169)

1716	Dryden 1.	Bod.
1723	Old Ballads 1.	U...C.
1724	Ever Green 1.	Bod.
1727	Dryden 3.	Bod.
1727	Old B 11 ds 4.	Bod.
1761	Ever Green 2.	Bod.
1769	Herd 1.	G.U.L.
1776	Herd 2.	Bod.
1777-84	Evans, Thomas, ed. Old Ballads. 4 vols. London, 1777-84.	Bod.
1783	A Select Collection of English Songs. 3 vols. London, 1783.	E.M.
1784	Caw, G., ed. The Poetical Museum. Hawick, 1784.	Bod.
1790	Morison, R., ed. A Select Collection of Favourite Scotish Ballads. 4 vols. Perth, 1790.	Bod.
1791	Herd 3.	Bod.
1794	[Ritson, Joseph, ed.] Scotish Songs. 2 vols. London, 1794.	Bod.
1796	Chapbooks, A Right Merrie Book of Garlands and Songs, "The 1st Good night of the Valiant Johny Armstrong". Aberdeen, 1796.	Bod.

JOHNNY ARMSTRONG'S LAST GOOD-NIGHT, see under JOHNIE
ARMSTRONG (169)

JOHNIE FAA, see under THE GYPSY LADDIE (200)

JOHNSTON HEY AND YOUNG CALDWELL, see under YOUNG JOHNSTONE

JOLLY BEGGAR (279)

Mill gives Herd's text of 1769 as "the first in any printed collection", but states that it was probably in circulation as "a flying-sheet". It was printed in The Goldfinch, 1753, doubtless from a flying-sheet.

1750c.   Chapbook, The Forsaken Lover's Garland.

1753   The Goldfinch. Glasgow, 1753.

1769   Herd 1.

1776   Herd 2.

1783   Pinkerton, John, ed. Select Scotish Ballads. London, 1783.

1737-1803   Johnson, James, ed. The Scots Musical Museum. 6 vols. Edinburgh, 1787-1803. No. 266.

1794   [Ritson, Joseph, ed.] Scotish Songs. 2 vols. London, 1794.

1750c.   Chapbooks, "The Jovial Tinker and Farmer's Daughter", "The Tinker and Farmer's Daughters Garland", "There was a Jolly Beggar".

TOMHA, see under TAM LIN (39)

KNIGHT AND LADY, see under THE FALSE KNIGHT (1

KNIGHT AND THE SHEPHERD'S DAUGHTER (110)

1764c.   Reliques 1.

1765   Reliques 2.

1767   Reliques 3.

1775   Reliques 4.

1794   Reliques 5.

ANNE BOTHWELL'S BALOW, see under LADY ANNE BOTHWELL'S LAMENT

ANNE BOTHWELL'S LAMENT

1706-11	Watson, James, ed. A Choice Collection of Comic and Serious Scots Poems both ancient and Modern. By Several Hands. Three parts in one volume. Edinburgh, 1706-11.	U.of
1726	Tea-Table 3.	N.L.S
1727	A New Miscellany of Scots Songs. London, 1727. (Ramsay's portrait opp. title page.)	Bod.
1730	Tea-Table 5.	Bod.
1733	Orpheus Caledonius 2.	Bod.
1740	Lark 1.	N.L.S
1740	Tea-Table 6.	Bod.
1742	Lark 2.	Bod.
1752	Charmer 2.	Bod.
1760	Tea-Table 7.	Bod.
1765	Charmer 3.	N.L.S
1765	Reliques 1.	U.of
1767	Reliques 3.	U.of
1768	A Collection of One Hundred and Fifty Scots Songs. London, 1768.	Bod.
1768	Tea-Table 8.	N.L.
1769	Herd 1.	G.U.L
1775	Reliques 4.	U.of
1776	Herd 2.	Bod.

1781	Pinkerton, John, ed. Scotish Tragic Ballads. London, 1781.	Bod.
1782	Charmer 4.	N.L.S
1782	Tea-Table 9.	U.of
1783	Pinkerton, John, ed. Select Scotish Ballads. London, 1783.	Bod.
1787-1803	Johnson, James, ed. The Scots Musical Museum. 6 vols. Edinburgh, 1787-1803. No. 130.	Bod.
1790	Morison, R., ed. A Select Collection of Favourite Scotish Ballads. 4 vols. Perth, 1790.	Bod.
1790	A Selection of the most favourite Scots Songs, chiefly pastoral. London, 1790.	Bod.
1791	Herd 3.	Bod.
1792	The Poetical Epitome or Elegant Extracts abridged. London, 1792.	B.M.
1794	Reliques 5.	Bod.
1794	[Ritson, Joseph, ed.] Scotish Song. 2 vols. London, 1794.	Bod.
1796	Elegant Extracts: or useful and entertaining Pieces of Poetry. London, 1796.	B.M.
1796	Chapbooks, Scotish Ballads and Songs. Manchester, 1796.	Bod.

LADY ISABEL AND THE ELF-KNIGHT (4)

1776	Herd 2.	Bod.
1790	Morison, R., ed. A Select Collection of favourite Scotish Ballads. 4 vols. Perth, 1790.	Bod.
1791	Herd 3.	Bod.

1750-1817   Chapbooks in Motherwell's Collec-
            tion, part of the Lauriston Castle
            Collection, "The Western Tragedy".

L MARY ANN, see under STILL GROWING

LADY TURND SERVING-MAN, see under THE FAMOUS
? SERVING-MAN (106)

LADY'S POLICY, see under THE BAFFLED KNIGHT (

LAILLY ORM, see under THE LAILY WORM AND TH
RCKREL OF THE SEA (36)

LAIDLEY WORM OF SPINDLESTON HAUGH, see under
AILY WORM AND THE MACKREL OF THE SEA (36)

LAILY WORM AND THE MACKREL OF THE SEA (36)

1777-84   Evans, Thomas, ed. Old Ballads.
            4 vols. London, 1777-84.

1793   [Ritson, Joseph, ed.] The North-
            umberland Garland; or Newcastle
            Nightingale, "The Laidley Worm of
            Spindleston Heugh". Newcastle, 17

1795   Chapbook in Maidment's Collection,
            "The Laidley Worm of Spindleston
            Heugh", "made by an old mountain
            bard, Duncan Frasier, living on
            Cheviot, A.D. 1270". Newcastle,
            1795.

1795   Chapbook in Maidment's Collection,
            Popular Poetry, "The Laidley Worm
            of Spindleston Heugh". Newcastle,
            1795.

L IRD OF GIGHT, or GA , see under GEORDIE (

LAIRD OF GIGH, or GAT, see under GEORDIE (709

L IRD O LIVINGSTONE, see under FAIR LADY OF
LLINGTON (91)

LAIRD O LOGI (182)

1769   Part 1.

| 1776 | Herd 2. | Bod. |

| 1790 | Morison, R., ed. A Select Collection of Favourite Scotish Ballads. 4 vols. Perth, 1790. | Bod. |

| 1794 | [Ritson, Joseph, ed.] Scotish Song. 2 vols. London, 1794. | Bod. |

| 1795c. | "The Laird of Logie", stall-copy. Stirling. | C.U.L |

BERT LINKIN, see under LAWKIN (93)

LAMENT OF THE BORDER WIDOW, see under THE FAMOUS FLOWER OF SERVING-MEN (106)

LAMENTATION OF HUGH GRAHAM, see under HUGHIE GRAEME (1?)

KIN (93)

| 1776 | Herd 2. | Bod. |

| 1790 | Morison, R., ed. A Select Collection of Favourite Scotish Ballads. 4 vols. Perth, 1790. | Bod. |

| 1791 | Herd 2. | Bod. |

LIKIN, see under LAWKIN (93)

LASS OF OCRAM, see under THE LASS OF ROCH ROYAN (76)

LASS OF ROCH ROYAN (76)

| 1776 | Herd 2. | Bod. |

| 1787-1803 | Johnson, James, ed. The Scots Musical Museum. 6 vols. Edinburgh, 1787-18??. No. 5. | Bod. |

| 1790 | Morison, R., ed. A Select Collection of Favourite Scotish Ballads. 4 vols. Perth, 1790. | Bod. |

| 1790-92 | Selection of the most favourite Scots Songs, chiefly pastoral. 2 vols. London, 1790-92. | Bod. |

1791	Herd 2.	Bod.
1792-1800	A Selection of Scots Songs, Harmonized and Improved with Simple, and Adapted Graces . . . by Peter Urbani, printed for the author of the music. Edinburgh, Glasgow, London, Dublin. 1792-1800.	Bod.
1799	Chapbook, J. and M. Robertson in the Saltmarket. Glasgow, 1799.	N.L.S.

THE LIFE AND DEATH OF SIR HUCH THE GRIME, see under HUGHIE GRAME (191)

THE LITTLE MAN, see under THE WEE WEE MAN (38)

LITTLE MUSGRAVE AND LADY BARNARD (81)

1716	Dryden 1.	Bod.
1727	Dryden 3.	Bod.
1764c.	Reliques 1.	Bod.
1765	Reliques 2.	U.of T
1767	Reliques 3.	U.of T
1775	Reliques 4.	U.of T
1794	Reliques 5.	Bod.

LIV'D AINCE TWA LOVERS IN YON DALE, see under FAIR JANET (64

LIZIE BAILLIE, see under BONNY LIZIE BAILLIE (227)

LIZIE LINDSAY (226)

Child makes no mention of any broadside or stall-copy of this ballad.

1777c.	Chapbook, "Lizie Lindsay". Edinburgh.	G.U.L.

LIZIE WAN (51)

1776	Herd 2.	Bod.

1790   Morison, R., ed. A Select Collection of Favourite Scotish Ballads.
4 vols. Perth, 1790.

THE LOCHMABEN HARPER (192)

 1787-1803 Johnson, James, ed. The Scots
     Musical Museum. 6 vols. Edinburgh,
     1787-1803. No. 579.

LORD GREGORY, see under THE LASS OF ROCH ROYAN (76)

LORD JOHN, see under THE BROOMFIELD HILL (43)

LORD JOHN'S MURDER, see under YOUNG JOHNSTONE (88)

LORD LIVINGSTON (262)

 1723   Old Ballads 1.

 1777   Old Ballads 4.

 1777-84 Evans, Thomas, ed. Old Ballads.
     4 vols. London, 1777-84.

 1781   Pinkerton, John, ed. Scotish Tragic
     Ballads. London, 1781.

LORD RANDAL (12)

 1787-1803 Johnson, James, ed. The Scots
     Musical Museum. 6 vols. Edinburgh,
     1787-1803. No. 327.

 1792-1800 A Selection of Scots Songs, Harmon-
     ized and Improved with Simple, and
     Adapted Graces . . . by Peter Urbani.
     Printed for the author of the music.
     Edinburgh, Glasgow, London, Dublin.
     1792-1800.

LORD RONALD MY SON, see under LORD RANDAL (12)

LORD RONALD'S DAUGHTER, see under CAPTAIN WEDDERBURN'S
 COURTSHIP (46)

LORD THOMAS AND FAIR ANNET (73)

 1723   Old Ballads 1.

1727	Old Ballads 4.	Bod.
1762 c.	Leaf nos 1, "Lord Thomas and Fair Annet" and "Lord Thomas and Fair Elliror".	Bod.
1765	Reliques 2, as in Reliques 1.	U.of
1767	Reliques 3, as in Reliques 1.	U.of
1768	A Collection of One Hundred and Fifty Scots Songs. London, 1768.	Bod.
1769	Herd 1.	G.U.L
1775	Reliques 4, as in Reliques 1.	U.of
1776	Herd 2.	Bod.
1783	A Select Collection of English Songs. 3 vols. London, 1783.	B.M.
1790	Morison, R., ed. A Select Collection of Favourite Scotish Ballads. 4 vols. Perth, 1790.	Bod.
1791	Herd 3.	Bod.
1794	Reliques 5, as in Reliques 1.	U.of
1794	[Ritson, Joseph, ed.] Scotish Songs. 2 vols. London, 1794.	Bod.
1794	Chapbook in Maidment's Collection, Popular Poetry, "The Goldfinch". 1794.	G.U.L
1795	Chapbook in Maidment's Collection, Popular Poetry, "Lord Thomas and Fair Annet". 1795.	G.U.L
1796	Chapbook, Scottish Ballads and Songs. Manchester, 1796.	Bod.
1798	Campbell, Alexander. An Introduction to the History of Poetry in Scotland . . . together with a conversation on Scottish Song . . . to which are subjoined Songs of the Lowlands of Scotland. Edin-	M.

____ ____ ____ ____ ____

1768	A ollection of ____ undr ____ ord "ift ots on s. Lon on, 1768.	_od.
1769	Herd 1.	.. ...
1776	Herd 2.	_od.
1787-1803	Johnson, James, e . The ots 'us cal useum. 6 vols. inbur ., 17 7-1 03. o. 114.	od.

1790-92   A selection of the most favourite
           Scots Songs, chiefly pastoral.
           London, 1790-92.

1791   Herd 2.

1794   [Ritson, Joseph, ed.] Scotish Song,
           "Macpherson's Farewell", and
           "Macpherson's Lament". 2 vols.
           London, 1794.

1798   Campbell, Alexander. An Introduc-
           tion to the History of Poetry in
           Scotland . . . . together with a
           conversation on Scotish Song . . . .
           to which are subjoined songs of the
           Lowlands of Scotland. Edinburgh,
           1798.

PHERSON'S LAMENT, see under MACPHERSON'S FAR L

PHERSON'S RANT, see under MACPHERSON'S FAREWELL

DEIL RIDDLE WISELY EXPOUNDED, see under RIDDLES
WISELY EXPOUNDED (1)

ORTHERN BALLAD, see under JOHNIE ARMSTRONG (169)

NORTHERN DITTY OR THE SCOTSMAN OUTWITTED BY THE
COUNTRY DAMSEL, see under THE BAFFLED KNIGHT (112

NUT BROWN BRIDE, see under LORD THOMAS AND FAIR
ANNET (73)

OLD YE WIFE OF KELLY BLIND HARPER, see under
OCHILBEN HARPER (192)

FIX THE DOOR LORD G GORY, see under THE LASS OF
ROYAN (76)

COOMAN (274)

1776   Herd 2.

1787-1803 Johnson, James, ed. The Scots
           Musical Museum. 6 vols. Edinburgh,
           1787-1803. No. 274.

1794   [Ritson, Joseph, ed.] Scottish Song.
            2 vols. London, 1794.

OUTLANDISH KNIGHT, see under LADY ISABEL AND THE
ELF-KNIGHT (4)

OVER-COURTEOUS KNIGHT, see under THE BAFFLED NI

NCE ROBERT (87)

Child has no broadside version of this. The copy
noted here has "An old Scottish Ballad (never befo
ublished.)"

1798   Chapbooks, Brash and Reid. Poetry
            original and selected. Glasgow, 1798.

EEN ELEANOR'S CONFESSION (156)

    1723   Old Ballads 1.

    1765   Reliques 2.

    1767   Reliques 3.

    1775   Reliques 4.

    1794   Reliques 5.

QUEEN OF ENGLAND, see under QUEEN ELEANOR'S
CONFESSION (156)

R. NTIN LADDIE (240)

1737-1803   Johnson, James, ed. The Scots
            Musical Museum. 6 vols. Edinburgh,
            1787-1803. No. 462.

WILLIE DROWND IN YARROW, or THE WATER O GAMRIE

    1733   Orpheus Caledonius 2.

    1734   The British Musical Miscellany of
                The Delightful Grove. London, 1734.

    1740   Tea-Table 6.

    1753   The Goldfinch. Glasgow, 1753.

1760	Tea-Table 7.	Bod.
1764	A Choice Collection of Scotch and English Songs taken from Marvllis, Phoenix, Orpheus, Charmer, Tea-Table, &c., &c., &c. Glasgow, 1764.	L.P.L.
1768	Tea-Table 8.	M.L.
1769	Herd 1.	G.U.L.
1776	Herd 2.	Bod.
1782	Tea-Table 8.	U.of T.
1787-1803	Johnson, James, ed. The Scots Music Museum. 6 vols. Edinburgh, 1787-1803. No. 525.	Bod.
1790	Morison, R., ed. A Select Collection of Favourite Scotish Ballads. 4 vols. Perth, 1790.	Bod.
1791	Herd 3.	Bod.
1794	[Ritson, Joseph, ed.] Scotish Songs. 2 vols. London, 1794.	Lo.
1796	Chapbooks, Scotish Ballads and Songs. Manchester, 1796.	Lo.

OLLEN WISELY EXPOUNDED (1)

1712	Durfey 1.	B.M.
1719	Durfey 2.	Bod.

N YOU MY FATHER, see under THE GREY COCK (248)

A SCOTCHMAN OUTWITTED, see under THE BAFFLED KNIGHT (112)

E'S PRICK'T HER EL AND PRIN'D IT WEL, see under TAM LIN (39)

1787-1803   Johnson, James, ed. The Scots
            Music 1 Museum. 6 vols. Edinburgh
            1787-1803. No. 461.

HE SHEPHERD'S SON, see under THE BAFFLED KNIGHT (

SILLY BLIND HARPER, see under THE LOCHMABEN HARP

IR ANDRE WOOD, see under SIR PATRICK SPENS (58)

IR JAMES THE ROSE (213)

In his notes on this ballad Child states that:
"Sir James the Ross' was first printed in The
Weekly Magazine, or the Edinburgh Amusement,
IX, 371, in 1770 . . . ."

This is not exact. The ballad appears in A
Collection of One Hundred and fifty Scots Songs,
London, 1768. It was reprinted in Ruddiman's
Weekly Magazine, or the Edinburgh Amusement,
September 1770, at which time Ruddiman said that
he gave the ballad from A Collection, minus the
ballad hawker's conclusion.

    1768   A Collection of One Hundred and
                fifty Scots Songs. London, 1768.

    1770   Ruddiman, T., ed. The Weekly
                Magazine, or The Edinburgh Amuse-
                ment, IX, September 1770.

    1774   The Annual Register, or View of
                the History, Politics and Litera-
                ture for the Year 1774. 4th ed.
                "The Buchanshire Tragedy; or Sir
                James the Ross". London, 1774.

    1776   Herd 2.

    1777-84   Evans, Thomas, ed. Old Ballads.
                4 vols. London, 1777-34.

    1781   Pinkerton, John, ed. Scotish
                Tragic Ballads. London, 1781.

    1783   Pinkerton, John, ed. Select
                Scotish Ballads. London, 1783.

18th Century Scottish Books, the catalogue of
e exhibition held at the Signet Library, Edin-
rgh, it is stated erroneously, pp.42-43, th t
nkerton's collection "is noteworthy for the
r_t appearance in print of _Sir James the Rose_"
nkerton's own notes state th t his version "is
ver from modern edition in one sheet . . .
ter the old copy".

1784   C.w, G., ed. _Th Poetic l Museum_,
            "Elfrid nd Sir James of Perth".
            H wick, 1784.

1785   Dro dsi e, "Sir James the Ross".
            dinburgh, 1785.

1785c.   Chapbook in L uri.ton C stle Colle
            tion, " ir Jam s the Ross".
            Stirling.

1790   orison, R., ed. _ elect Collec-
            tion of F vourite cotish B ll ds_.
            4 vols. Perth, 179 .

1791   _Herd_ 2.

1796   Chapbook., _ Si ht Merrie Book of
            G rl nd nd Song_, "The Buchan-
            shire Tr gedy, or ir J mes the
            Ross". Edinburgh, 1796.

1798   Chapbooks, Pr se nd Poid, _Poetry;
            origin l nd selected_. Gl s ow,179

1799   G rl nd of B ll ds, "The Buch n-
            shire Tragedy or ir J mes the Ros .
            P i ley, 1799.

1750-1800   Ch book in Motherwell's Collection
            p rt of L uriston C stle Collection
            " ir J m s the Ross".

J MES TH ROS , see un er IL J M Th O R (

JOHN G R EM ND RH R LLIN, see un er JOHN Y
GR   LL N (84)

P TTICK R M (58)
1765   _Reliques_ 2.

1767	Reliques 2.	U.of T.
1768	A Collection of One Hundred and Fifty Scots Songs. London, 1768.	Bod.
1769	Herd 1.	G.U.L.
1775	Reliques 4.	Bod.
1776	Herd 2.	Bod.
1781	Pinkerton, John, ed. Scotish Tragic Ballads. London, 1781.	Bod.
1783	Pinkerton, John, ed. Select Scotish Ballads. London, 1783.	Bod.
1787-1803	Johnson, James, ed. The Scots Musical Museum. 6 vols. Edinburgh, 1787-1803. No. 482.	Bod.
1790	Morison, R., ed. A Select Collection of Favourite Scotish Ballads. 4 vols. Perth, 1790.	Bod.
1791	Herd 3.	Bod.
1794	Reliques 5.	Bod.
1794	[Ritson, Joseph, ed.] Scotish Songs. 2 vols. London, 1794.	Bod.

SIR ROBERT BEWICK AND THE LAIRD GRAHAM, see under
BEWICK AND GRAHAM (211)

STILL GROWING

1787-1803	Johnson, James, ed. The Scots Musical Museum. 6 vols. Edinburgh, 1787-1803. No. 377.	Bod.

SWEET WILLIAM AND MAY MARGARET, see under SWEET
WILLIAM'S GHOST (77)

SWEET WILLIAM AND THE YOUNG COLONEL, see under YOUNG
JOHNSTONE (88)

1764	A Choice Collection of Scotch and English Songs taken from Amaryllis, Phoenix, Orpheus, Charmer, Tea-Table, &c., &c., &c. Glasgow, 1764.	S.P.L.
1765	Charmer 3.	N.L.S.
1765	Lark 3.	N.L.S.
1765	Reliques 2.	U. of T
1767	Reliques 3.	U. of T
1768	Tea-Table 8.	M.L.
1769	Herd 1.	G.U.L.
1775	The Caledoniad. A Collection of Poems, written chiefly by Scottish authors. London, 1775.	Bod.
1775	Reliques 4.	U. of T
1776	Herd 2.	Bod.
1780	The Chearfull Companion, containing a Select Collection of Favourite Scots and English Songs, Catches &c., many of which are originals. Perth, 1780.	S.P.L.
1782	Charmer 4.	N.L.S.
1782	Tea-Table 9.	U. of T
1783	Pinkerton, John, ed. Select Scotish Ballads. London, 1783.	Bod.
1787-1803	Johnson, James, ed. The Scots Musical Museum. 6 vols. Edinburgh, 1787-1803. No. 250.	Bod.
1790	Morison, R., ed. A Select Collection of Favourite Scottish Ballads. 4 vols. Perth, 1790.	Bod.

1790	Ramsay, Allan. Thirty Scots Songs, adapted for a voice and harpsichord by Robert Bremner. London, 1790.	M.L
1791	Herd 3.	Bod
1792-1800	A Selection of Scots Songs, harmonized and Improved, with Simple and Adapted Graces . . . by Peter Urbani. Printed for the author of the music. Edinburgh, Glasgow, London, Dublin, 1792-1800.	Bod
1794	Reliques 5.	Bod
1794	[Ritson, Joseph, ed.] Scotish Song. 2 vols. London, 1794.	Bod
1795c.	Dale's Collection of sixty favourite Scotch Songs, taken from the original Manuscripts of the most celebrated Scotch Authors and Composers. London.	Bod
1796	Chapbooks, Scotish Ballads and Songs. Manchester, 1796.	Bod
1798	Campbell, Alexander. An Introduction to the History of Poetry in Scotland . . . together with a conversation on Scotish Song ... to which are subjoined Songs of the Lowlands of Scotland. Edinburgh, 1798.	E.U

GLEN, see under TAM LIN (39)

A-LINE, THE ELFIN KNIGHT, see under TAM LIN (39)

ANF, see under TAM LIN (39)

LIN (39)

| 1769 | Herd 1. | G.U. |
| 1776 | Herd 2. | Bod. |

[...]
... t e time o ...
Third to ...

...
(1)

1727	_ry, en 2._	Bod.
1781	Pinkerton, John, ed. <u>Scottish Tragic Ballads.</u> London, 1781.	Bo .
1783	Pinkerton, John, ed. <u>Select Scottish Ballads.</u> London, 1783.	Bod.
1790	Morison, R., ed. <u>A Select Collection of Favourite Scotish Ballads.</u> 4 vols. Perth, 1790.	Bod.
1791	<u>Herd 3.</u>	Bod.

FAIR SISTERS, see under THE T A SIST (10)

UNCO KNICHT'S WOOING, see under RIDDLE FINELY KPOUNDED (1)

D' WALE' UP YON BANK

1725	<u>Orpheus Caledonius 1.</u>	Bod.
1726	<u>Tea-Table 2.</u>	N.L...
1727	<u>A New Miscellany of Scots Songs.</u> London, 1727. (Ramsay's portrait opp. title page.)	Bod.
1730	<u>Tea-Table 5.</u>	Bod.
1733	<u>Orpheus Caledonius 2.</u>	Bod.
1740	<u>Lark 1.</u>	N.L...
1740	<u>Tea-Table 6.</u>	Bod.
1742	<u>Lark 2.</u>	Bod.
1751	<u>Charmer 1.</u>	Bod.
1757	<u>Thirty Scots Songs for a Voice and Harpsichord. The Music taken from the most genuine Set, extant; the words from Allan Ramsay. Edinburgh, 1757.</u>	N.L.

1760	Tea-Table 7.	Bod.
1764	A Choice Collection of Scotch and English Songs taken from Amaryllis, Phoenix, Orpheus, Charmer, Tea-Table, &c., &c., &c. Glasgow, 1764.	.P.L
1764c.	Reliques 1.	Bod.
1765	Charmer 3.	N.L.S
1765	Lark 3.	N.L.S
1765	Reliques 2.	U.of
1767	Reliques 3.	U.of
1768	A Collection of One Hundred and Fifty Scots Songs. London, 1768.	Bod.
1768	Tea-Table 8.	M.L.
1769	Herd 1.	G.U.L
1775	The Caledoni d. A Collection of Poems written chiefly by Scottish authors. London, 1775.	Bod.
1775	Reliques 4.	U.of
1776	Herd 2.	Bod.
1782	Charmer 4.	N.L.S
1782	Tea-Table 9.	U.of
1783	The Blackbird, a new edition. Berwick, 1783.	Bod.
1784	Chapbook in Maidment's Collection. The Dairy Maid etc. 1784.	G.U.L
1787-1803	Johnson, James, ed. The Scots Musical Museum. 6 vols. Edinburgh, 1787-1803. No. 158.	Bod.

1787-88	A Collection of Scots Songs, "Thirty Scots Songs . . . The Words by Allan Ramsey". Edinburgh, 1787-88.
1790	Morison, R., ed. A Select Collection of Favourite Scotish Ballads. 4 vols. Perth, 1790.
1790	Ramsay, Allan. Thirty Scots Songs, adapted for a voice and harpsichord by Robert Bremner. London, 1790.
1790-92	A Selection of the most favourite Scots Songs, chiefly pastoral. 2 vols. London, 1790-92.
1791	Herd 3.
1792-1800	A Selection of Scots Songs, Harmonized and Improved with Simple, and Adapted Graces . . . by Peter Urbani. Edinburgh, Glasgow, London, Dublin, 1792-1800.
1794	Reliques 5.
1794	[Ritson, Joseph, ed.] Scotish Song. 2 vols. London, 1794.
1795c.	Dale's Collection of Sixty favourite Scotch Songs, taken from the original Manuscripts of the most Celebrated Scotch Authors and Composers. London.
1798	Campbell, Alexander. Introduction to the History of Poetry in Scotland . . . together with a conversation on Scotish Song . . . to which are subjoined Songs of the Lowlands of Scotland. Edinburgh, 1798.
1798c.	Chapbook, Brash and Reid. Poetry; original and selected, "O waly, waly &c." Glasgo..
1750-1800	Chapbook in Motherwell's Collection,

ALY, ALY, GIN LOVE BE BOTTY, see under ALE' AL
YON BANK

ALY, ALY, UP THE BANK, see under ALE' ALE' UP
BANK

A WARNING PIECE TO ENGLAND AGAINST PRIDE AND WICKE
NESS, see under QUEEN ELINOR'S CONFESSION (156)

WATER O CARY, see under RARE WILLIE DROWNED IN
YARROW (215)

WATER O GAMRIE, see under RARE WILLIE DROWNED IN
YARROW (215)

WATER O GAMRIE, see under RARE WILLIE DROWNED IN
YARROW (215)

THE WATER O' WEARIE'S WELL, see under LADY ISABEL A
ELF-KNIGHT (4)

THE WEE WEE MAN (38)

    1776   Herd 2.

    1784   Caw, G., ed. The Poetical Museum.
           Hawick, 1784.

    1787-1803 Johnson, James, ed. The Scots
           Musical Museum. 6 vols. Edinburgh,
           1787-1803. No. 382.

    17901790 Morison, R., ed. A Select Collection
           of Favourite Scotish Ballads. 4 vols
           Perth, 1790.

    17911791 Herd 2.

    1794   [Ritson, Joseph, ed.] Scotish Song.
           2 vols. London, 1794

1761	Ever Green 2.	Bod.
1769	Herd 1.	G.U.L.
1770	Ancient Scottish Poems, published from M S. of George Bannatyne. MDLXVIII. Edinburgh, 1770.	Bod.
1776	Herd 2.	Bod.
1783	Pinkerton, John, ed. Select Scotish Ballads. London, 1783.	Bod.
1785	[Ritson, Joseph, ed.] The Caledonian Muse, a chronological selection of Scotish Poetry from the earliest times. London, 1785. (Printed 1785, published 1821.)	Bod.
1787-1803	Johnson, James, ed. The Scots Musical Museum. 6 vols. Edinburgh, 1787-1803. No. 595.	Bod.
1790	Morison, R., ed. A Select Collection of Favourite Scotish Ballads. 4 vols. Perth, 1790.	Bod.
1791	Herd 3.	Bod.
1750-1812	Chapbook in Motherwell's Collection, part of Lauriston Castle Collection.	N.L.S.

WILL YE GO TO THE HIELANS?   see under GEORDIE (209)

WILLIAM AND MARGARET, see under FAIR MARGARET AND SWEET WILLIAM (74)

WILLIAM AND MARJORIE, see under SWEET WILLIAM'S GHOST (77)

WILLIE AND ANNET, see under FAIR JANET (64)

WILLIE AND JANET, see under FAIR JANET (64)

WILLIE DOO, see under LORD RANDAL (12)

WILLIE'S DROWNED IN GAMERY, see under RARE WILLIE DROWNED IN YARROW (215)

WILLIE'S DROWNED IN **YARROW**, see under RARE WILLIE DROWNED
IN YARROW (215)

WILLIE O WINSBURY (100)

    1795   Chapbook in Motherwell's Collection,
                   part of Lauriston Castle Collection,
                   Ballads, "Lord Thomas of Winsbury's
                   Courtship". 1795.   N.L.S.

WILLY'S RARE AND WILLY'S FAIR, see under RARE WILLIE
DROWNED IN YARROW (215)

YOUNG BEICHAN (53)

    1785c.   Chapbook in Lauriston Castle Collec-
                   tion, "Susan Py: or Young Beichen's
                   Garland". Stirling.   N.L.S.

YOUNG JOHNSTONE (88)

    1769   Herd 1.   G.U.L.

    1776   Herd 2.   Bod.

    1779   Chapbook in Maidment's Collection,
                   Popular Poetry, Miscellaneous
                   Ballads, "The Cruel Knight". Edin-
                   burgh, 1779.   G.U.L.

    1783   John Pinkerton, ed. Select Scottish
                   Ballads. London, 1783.   Bod.

    1791   Herd 3.   Bod.

    1794   [Ritson, Joseph, ed.] Scotish Song.
                   2 vols. London, 1794.   Bod.

THE YOUNG LAIRD OF OCHILTREE, see under THE LAIRD O
LOGIE (182)

THE YOUNG TAMLANE, see under TAM LIN (39)

YOUNG WATERS (94)

    1755   Chapbook printed by Robert and Andrew
                   Foulis, "Young Waters, An Ancient
                   Scottish Poem, never before printed".
                   Glasgow, 1755.   M.L.

1765	_Reliques 2._	U.of T.
1767	_Reliques 3._	U.of T.
1768	_A Collection of One Hundred and Fifty Scots Songs._ London, 1768.	Bod.
1769	_Herd 1._	G.U.L.
1775	_Reliques 4._	U.of T.
1776	_Herd 2._	Bod.
1791	_Herd 3._	Bod.
1794	_Reliques 5._	Bod.
1794	[Ritson, Joseph, ed.] _Scotish Song._ 2 vols. London, 1794.	Bod.